A RIGHT AMBITION

Books by David Gower

ANYONE FOR CRICKET
(with Bob Taylor)

TIME TO SPARE
(with Alan Lee)

HEROES AND CONTEMPORARIES
(with Derek Hodgson)

A
RIGHT
AMBITION

David Gower
with Derek Hodgson

*'If you have a right ambition you will
desire to excel all boys at cricket
. . . as well as in learning'*

Lord Chesterfield, to his son

COLLINS
8 Grafton Street, London W1
1986

William Collins Sons and Co Ltd
London · Glasgow · Sydney · Auckland
Toronto · Johannesburg

BRITISH LIBRARY CATALOGUING IN PUBLICATION DATA

Gower, David
A right ambition.
1. Cricket
I. Title   II. Hodgson, Derek
796.35'8'0924   GV917

ISBN 0 00 217043 4

Photoset in Linotron Imprint by
Rowland Phototypesetting Ltd
Bury St Edmunds, Suffolk
Made and Printed in Great Britain by
William Collins Sons and Co Ltd, Glasgow

Contents

Illustrations

All the pictures are by Patrick Eagar [PE],
Jan Traylen [JT] and David Munden [DM].

Between pages 32 and 33

Gundappa Viswanath: Concentration, eye on the ball, moving into position. [PE]

Geoffrey Boycott: Forward defensive, killing the spin. [PE]

Martin Crowe: The off-drive. [JT]

The off-drive, almost straight. [PE]

Imran Khan: The on-drive. [PE]

Ian Botham: Lofted straight drive. [PE]

Clive Lloyd: The square drive. [PE]

Allan Border: Another square drive. [PE]

Barry Richards: Timing a cut. [PE]

Mohinder Amarnath: Dancing into the cut. [PE]

Vivian Richards: Late cutting. [JT]

The cut completed, the run called, the ball should be beating third man. [PE]

The pull, as seen by the keeper. [PE]

The pull, as seen by the bowler who wishes he hadn't. [PE]

A pull-drive, sometimes described as a 'lap-shot' for fairly obvious reasons. [PE]

Gordon Greenidge: Hooking. [PE]

Mike Gatting: The sweep. [PE]

Between pages 64 and 65

Richard Ellison: Swing is king. [PE]

Les Taylor: Tireless, accurate, underestimated. [PE]

Craig McDermott: Tiger, tiger, learning fast. [PE]

Philippe Edmonds: Theoretician. [PE]
Abdul Qadir: Pick this one if you can. [PE]
Sivaramakrishnan: Moody. [PE]
Roger Harper: The man with the longer arm. [PE]
Eden Gardens, Calcutta – one of the world's great
   cricket grounds. [PE]
Sunil Gavaskar: A powerful cover drive. [PE]
Paul Downton: Natural talent, high ability. [PE]
'Can he manage another burst from the top end?' Actually I'm
   undertaking respiratory training from the Red Cross. [DM]
Vice captain Peter Willey and the Benson and Hedges Cup,
   captured by the Running Fox. [DM]
With A.R.B. – good friend, good bloke, great player. [DM]
The straight drive towards 215, Fifth Test, Edgbaston, 1985. [PE]
The secret is to let 'Both' do it his own way. [DM]
England: All the bright company, 1985. [PE]
England: It was a good vintage. [PE]

Preface
by David Gower

The origins of this book lie in its predecessor, *Heroes and Contemporaries*, published by my good friends at Collins in 1983. It was then felt that these present memoirs and observations would represent an interim collection of writings before I embark upon the story of my complete cricketing career.

There is such intense interest in the lives and performances of public figures that one would need to be a recluse of hermit-like proclivity to avoid revealing personal details, opinions and beliefs. The trick is to try to satisfy that interest without leaving oneself entirely naked and I have not, as far as I know, committed myself in this book on race, religion, sex, politics or on the cricket correspondents of popular newspapers. *A Right Ambition* starts where every book on cricket should begin, with a small boy's wish to wield a bat. It ends, like all good fairy stories, with that small boy having grown up to join an England team which won back the Ashes from Australia and with his joy and delight at having been able to play the game in so many wonderful places and to have made so many lasting friends.

The first part of the book deals much with technique, my own practice and methods being compared with

9

those of a selection of past masters. The book I grew up with was Sir Donald Bradman's *The Art of Cricket* (Hodder and Stoughton, 1958). Derek Hodgson then extended the Bibliography by including *W. G., the Cricketing Reminiscences of W. G. Grace* (republished by the Hambledon Press in 1980), Ranjitsinjhi's *Jubilee Book of Cricket* (Blackwood, 1897) and *Geoff Boycott on Batting* (Stanley Paul, 1980). If W. G. and Ranji seem impossibly distant figures to younger readers then they should be reminded that most cricket historians regard both as the originals; they defined the art of batting, laid down the rules and were as influential in their chosen field as Mozart or Chuck Berry. All batsmen since, even Viv Richards and Ian Botham, brilliant extrapolators both, owe much to the Old Man and to the Prince.

Bradman cannot be left out of any reference to batting, representing as he does the ultimate extension in technique. Of all contemporary players Boycott is outstanding in his length of occupation of the crease, scoring heavily on all pitches and in all parts of the world – he is the painstaking guardian of technical proficiency, the unblinking custodian of the nets, the supreme professional.

Cricket has changed at a faster rate in the past 25 years than at any time in its history. I like to think of myself as very much a modern player, one who entered the game when one-day matches were already established and popular. I have written before that I cannot see any real objection to tastefully-coloured players' uniforms, or even the use of numbers, if they help the public to identify with and enjoy the game. After all, our famous ancestors were known to play in coloured sashes and polka dots! But there are influences and practices creeping into the game that do little for its prestige or dignity and I hope that *A Right Ambition* will also serve as one opinion on these matters. There is very little wrong with first-class cricket today nor, I suspect, has there been much wrong with it in the past but that is because it has always been jealously guarded, certainly in England, where cricket-lovers have kept a wary eye on potential manipulators.

On a more personal note I have sketched the men batsmen fear today, a 'hit list', if you like, of the world's top bowlers. Almost all, I'm pleased to say, are friends of mine and the fact that I occasionally take a few runs off them or they have me caught behind in no way lessens that amity.

Friendship, and the respect that entails, lie at the heart of a successful team. Dressing-room rivalries there will always be and it is the captain's task to see that even the fiercest competitor subordinates his own ambition to the team's cause. A winning team is a balanced and blended team and the coming together of England in the years 1982–85 is an important part of *A Right Ambition*.

DAVID GOWER
Leicester, December 1985

PART I

'To Excel All Boys'

Lord Chesterfield

The first part of this book is essentially for the younger reader and the player who likes to be comforted by the discovery that he is not unique in finding it difficult to play certain shots and to deal with some bowlers.

The masterstrokes are here, for we all have to learn from the masters; where conditions and circumstances have changed I have tried to make my own contribution to the debate.

THE BAT

The bat is the basic tool of the trade. No doubt there are those at either end of the scale to whom the particular bat used makes precious little difference, but to the great majority of players confidence in their chosen weapon is one of the most important facets of their game. It matters not how much training and practice you put into your game if at the crucial moment you are going to be let down by the piece of wood in your hands. You must be confident that if you connect with the ball properly it will go as far and as fast in the right direction as you wish it to go. It's no good trying to hit the ball properly with a bat that is as dead as the proverbial railway sleeper, and certainly no professional player or any amateur with suitable pride in his performance will tolerate a bat like that for too long.

The first bat that I can remember my parents buying for me – they actually took me out for the specific purpose of buying a bat – was when I was at prep school in Kent. It was a Ken Barrington Autograph that was treasured, cared for, oiled lovingly and it was the bat with which I scored my first century when I was 12. Here was a bat that could do no wrong in my young eyes and it was, no doubt, the most treasured possession of my life up to then. I used it for two or three years. It ended up a true veteran, brown and bound with string and greatly honoured. Sad to say, as I grew out of that bat it was soon enough relegated to garden cricket and I made do through my early years at King's Canterbury with the odd bits and pieces supplied by the school, until I was finally chosen for the First XI and asked my parents for a new bat of my own. I was presented with a brand new Gray-Nicholls which stood me in good stead through the next couple of years – again as things seemed to be going reasonably well the bat was endowed with complete respect.

That was the start of an uninterrupted association with Gray-Nicholls which continues to this day. It goes without saying that at that stage they were unlikely to have envisaged this relationship, but when I first began playing for Leicestershire II I was eventually offered two bats for the price of one, which seemed a good deal and one which I was happy to accept. In time I was fortunate enough to be offered their sponsorship which, as will be obvious, was preaching to the converted. I have enjoyed a fruitful partnership with them ever since. By now we have reached the stage where Gray-Nicholls know the specifications I seek in a bat so that they have a basic structure to work upon when they are seeking to make improvements. At the start of a season I ask to try a number of bats and they, in turn, send one or two unasked to see what I think of them. Occasionally I revise my specifications or perhaps I will experiment with a suggestion from them: it's a continuing dialogue, really, with both the batmakers and myself seeking that particular piece of wood that will guarantee me 3,000 runs a season, every season.

I would not wish to discourage anyone who, having read the last paragraph, may think that one needs to be a Test player in order to get the best bat, or even a good bat. The simple truth about bats is that a good one can come from anywhere. Much skill goes into making the most expensive bats but it is a fact that the best willow, workmanship and care cannot guarantee the best bat. As with almost everything in cricket, luck is a factor and you can get some excellent bats from what is supposed to be two- or three-star wood.

Geoff Boycott says that a bat is 'very much a matter of personal preference' and that is illustrated by a story told by W. G. Grace about the old Lancashire professional who retired to run a sports shop where one day a customer sought to buy a bat he described as a 'slipper'. Asked to explain the man replied: 'Well, I want a bat that I can guide the ball through the slips with'. Convinced he was dealing with what we would today call a total wally, the old professional sold the man a thin-bladed, ill-balanced bat that he had been reluctant, indeed unable, to sell. At the end of that summer the shopkeeper was a little alarmed to see the customer returning but the man beamed and said he was delighted, adding, 'That's the best bat I've ever handled'.

There have always been fashions in bats, different shapes, sizes and weights, but with all of them the same rules apply: there will be good bats and bad bats and the best is the one that suits you. When Gray-Nicholls send me a half-dozen bats each spring I select two or three to use. They have to be broken in and I start playing with the one I feel is nearest to being ready for use, take another that is less advanced and needs more playing in, and sometimes I carry a third as a spare, hoping that all of them will be of a suitable quality to meet my special requirements. However, it is not always the bat that is at fault when you decide to change. When runs are scarce, you may feel you need a change of luck so you discard one bat and take up another, although common sense tells you there is absolutely nothing wrong with the first bat. But, of course, it works.

I can remember one spectacular change in my performance. In 1979 I had a poor start to my Leicestershire season; I could hardly get a run. The Indians came to Leicester and I didn't do too well against them, either, so I took out a complete new set of kit for the First Test at Edgbaston – new pads, gloves and bat – and scored 200. That is the sort of occasion on which I can say, 'Yes, I believe in superstition'. As far as I am concerned, you should make superstition work for you, but as soon as it fails, discard it, forget it. Don't take it seriously unless it is working for you. Of course, superstition in this sense is merely but nonetheless importantly a question of giving yourself an extra mental boost when you are walking out to the crease, just topping up your confidence, and it is not a great idea to become over-dependent on your little foibles.

While we are on the subject, it was, coincidentally, another change of bat in the summer of 1985 that preceded a notable improvement in my luck and a few runs against the Australians. When the second bat broke at Edgbaston during the Fifth Test, rival manufacturer but friend Duncan Fearnley was on hand to take it back to his factory, effect immediate repairs, and make sure the bat was ready for the Sixth Test as well, during which it produced suitable results!

Certain other little habits can make good common sense – for instance, I normally take bats that need knocking in with me to the nets, rather than make too many demands of the old faithful that I am relying on out in the middle and wish to preserve. Preparing for either a season or a winter tour I usually have a mixture of suitably knocked-in and new bats. It is not always desirable to take a brand new bat out to the middle with you but usually a top quality bat should not let you down. However, it is very much worth noting that the more one is prepared to break in a bat the longer it is likely to last and repay you for time well spent in its preparation.

As far as weight is concerned, I use a bat of about 2lb 8oz to 2lb 10oz. The average weight 20 years ago was around 2lb 3oz while most batsmen today are using bats that are 2lb 10oz upwards. Historical comparisons are interesting: Bradman always used a bat of about 2lb 4oz. W. G. Grace commented: 'I never saw a good cutter use a heavy bat. I play with a bat weighing about two pounds five which I think is heavy enough for anybody'. One of the most prodigious modern scorers,

Boycott, favours 2lb 6oz. Today many batsmen use three-pounders, the heavy bat being definitely in vogue. Yet weight in itself is not decisive in terms of pick-up – two bats of identical weight can pick up quite differently. Many of the heavy bats used by my colleagues feel much the same in the back lift as one of my own. It's also possible to lift a bat that a team-mate has scored hundreds of runs with and feel as though you are lifting concrete. You cannot imagine how anyone could possibly play shots with such a monster.

As a general rule, the young player should not buy a bat that is too big or too heavy. Choose a bat that feels free and easy to wield; do not overtax either your strength or your technique. When you pick up a bat in the shop do not buy it, and do not let your parents buy it, unless you are convinced that it feels right. Grace put it this way: 'Style is ease and ease is strength. The most stylish players are, as a rule, good players; practise with a stick or broom handle and a soft ball. As boys grow up they should be provided with bats according to their style of play. A hard hitter will want a heavier bat or at all events a heavier bat than a batsman who plays quietly'. And a right-hander, Boycott, put it very succinctly, 'Your bat should be an extension of your left arm'.

Finally, take care of your bat. Ranji advised that your bat should be rubbed over with a rag well soaked in oil two or three times a week during the summer and twice a month in the winter. Bradman warns against oiling too frequently, adding, 'If your bat becomes wet rub it over with a light sandpaper and then oil'. Ranji also reminded us, 'Good workmen usually have good tools and, what is more, take care of them'. Nowadays of course many bats have protective surfaces that preclude oiling, but if you still prefer (or can find!) basic, dependable willow it will appreciate the attention you bestow upon it. Beware too much attention though, as over-oiling does little good: a couple of light coats to start with, and then a further very light coat after cleaning with fine sandpaper should see the bat through nicely.

COACHING

My first coach was my father. He was a very good schoolboy cricketer and, as I remember him, I feel sure he would have been a University cricketer too, had he not felt it necessary to work very hard academically through the summer terms. He did get a hockey Blue at Cambridge, confirming my memory of him as a versatile player of many sports.

It certainly has to be the best and biggest encouragement for a young aspirant when his or her parents take a serious interest, and both my father and my mother spent time in those early years bowling at the young Gower in the back garden for hours on end. It helps, of course, if at the same time some sort of technique is taught, whether by the parents or by a professional coach. Neither a parent nor every coach is guaranteed to give all the right advice, and genuinely good coaches at all levels are not easily found. I am very lucky in that all through my school career there were people with good cricketing common sense to guide me in the right direction, without being over-restrictive or trying to coach out my natural abilities, and in that nobody at any stage became too overbearing to kill my natural enthusiasm for the game. It must always be remembered that the game is to be enjoyed as well as played and that coaching should be aimed at increasing that enjoyment.

While one is naturally likely to receive advice from all quarters, it is always useful if at all possible to see for yourself what you look like with bat in hand; and for starters you can simply find a suitable mirror in front of which to practise a few shots. I hope it goes without saying that to use a full-size cricket bat without great care in these circumstances could lead to minor disasters and a minimum seven years' bad luck. The old masters believed in the mirror drill. Ranji, in advising a boy (and, nowadays, a girl) to acquire a style that is 'safe, sound and effective', went on: 'Harry Jupp is said to have practised daily in front of a looking-glass in order to make sure of playing with a straight bat. He had a chalk line on the floor and used to swing his bat up and down it'. In fact neither Grace nor Bradman, as films prove, took the bat back perfectly straight but, crucially, the bat was absolutely right when it addressed the ball.

Nowadays the 'looking-glass' may be old hat for youngsters, or at least for the fortunate few who have the opportunity to see themselves practise on home video. How it's done is unimportant as long as you are able to see yourself playing shots. Test players see themselves all too often on television and there is no lack of advice when things go wrong, but I accept that these films are valuable, instructional and often salutary.

It is very important to see exactly where you are putting your feet when playing a certain shot; how you are standing, how you lift the bat and how you bring it down. It is possible, now, for the novice to spot and eradicate most of the basic errors by simply watching and learning from a video film. I appreciate that not everyone can afford video facilities, or has access to them, but this is a form of coaching that schools and clubs should consider very seriously. Don't be depressed if for one reason or another video is denied to you. There are very many talented, high-class batsmen around the world who haven't seen all that much television, never mind video films.

What does no harm either is to watch the top-class players on every possible occasion, live or on film. Don't miss the chance to see innings by Graham Gooch, Ian Botham, Viv Richards or Allan Border, and note the apparent ease with which the game can be played, before trying to appreciate the many technical elements that all have to be put together over the years to achieve that ease. By all means try to emulate them but before you do try to play shots like Graham and Ian, remember that those shots can be played properly only as an extension of a correct basic technique, and that until you have mastered that technique yourself you would be better employed playing the simple, straightforward textbook strokes. As a boy I loved to watch the great left-handers, Pollock, Sobers and Edrich, three different temperaments and three very different styles. I cannot say now that I play like any one of them and that is because over the years my own style has developed, a projection of my own physique, temperament and learning, yet I have always been conscious of wishing to emulate them. Idols are necessary both as an example and as a target.

Whatever your age and whatever your standard of play there is always room for improvement. Self-correction is a continuing process. I remain fascinated by batsmen I admire and would have no qualms about stealing a little method from them if I thought it would improve my own game. I would emphasise in that statement the words 'I thought'. Cricket is very much a mental game as well as a physical one, and your confidence is all-important to what you are intending to do on the cricket field. All three aspects of the game, batting, bowling and fielding, become harder if your confidence is low – if you have not made a run, taken a wicket or held a catch in three weeks – and again this affects the top players just as much as those of lesser ability. From the batsman's point of view, that little extra hesitancy means that the feet move fractionally too late, the bat comes down in the wrong place and you start trying to play your shots at the wrong time, with the predictable disastrous results.

At times like these one always has to struggle through, perhaps trying to keep things as simple as possible, curbing one's natural ambition, cutting out all risks, and resisting the temptation to hit the next ball for four to try to restore that confidence in one blow. Sometimes it works – sometimes. Equally, if you can struggle through that initial part of the innings things can start to sort themselves out and all that ability you thought had disappeared for good suddenly comes back to you. Of course, when all is rosy and confidence is high the whole game seems different and much easier. I have only to look back at my own fortunes in the 1985 Ashes series to remember the differences between making 3 and 0 in the first one-day international and finishing with 157 at The Oval in the last Test match. One simply believes that whatever one does will work and that bowlers cannot bowl, and the only danger here is over-confidence, which can lead to one's downfall as fast as lack of it.

How do you measure confidence? I wish I knew. It goes up and down; you have to weather the bad patches and make the most of the good, play the percentages, as the Americans say. 'Make the most of it when the wheel of fortune comes round to you', as Graham Gooch puts it. It could be said that once you have passed a certain level in natural ability and technical training most of what remains in the game amounts to confidence and its application, so it is wise to use every means to increase that confidence. The great South African, Barry Richards, a magnificent batsman, was one who worked on his game until there was little left to chance. He would practise one shot for hours, with a bowler putting the ball where he needed it, until he had that one stroke 'grooved' into his repertoire. If and when Barry detected a weakness – perhaps his timing was awry, or his direction was amiss, or he felt that he was suffering a high percentage of dismissals from playing a certain shot – then it would be back to the drawing-board for more hard work until he was satisfied that if the ball arrived in a certain way then he would have the perfectly-controlled response to it. The moral is: never waste time in practice by just going out to the nets and whacking the ball around. Use the time properly, analyse your game, work on what needs strengthening.

Geoffrey Boycott is the perfect model for the learning batsman, a man who has never been too proud to practise hard and frequently. One of his early methods was to drill a hole through a composition ball, attach it by a wire to an overhanging branch or beam so that it hung just below waist-level and then practise swinging the bat through the ball. If the correct contact is made then the ball will return to its original position for you to hit it again and again. Conversely, if you are not addressing the ball correctly it will fly off at an angle.

Boycott also has some wise words on net practice. He prefers to have no more than three bowlers, believing that a greater number produces a battery of deliveries that allows no time for the batsman to think out what he is doing with each shot. If you have to practise alone Boycott suggests you strengthen your left arm and wrist by holding the bat in your left hand only, dropping the ball with your right hand and driving it into the net first bounce.

'It must be remembered that a great amount of labour, even drudgery, is required before a man can become a really good player', wrote Ranji in the last century. The greatest of them all, Bradman, who also compiled a very fine instructional book, *The Art of Batting*, practised with a stump and golf ball. This, by minimising the margin for error, naturally helps you learn the art of watching the ball for as long as possible before the moment of impact until, you hope, the process becomes automatic. Thus squash is an excellent game for cricketers, testing your reactions and mobility with that same vital emphasis on the golden rule of all such games: keep your eye on the ball. In squash it is impossible to take your eye away from such a small ball travelling very quickly; you have to watch it to the very end, right until it reaches the racquet, a useful exercise in concentration.

When things are not going well in cricket it is often the case that the batsman is simply ignoring the golden rule and not watching the ball all the way on to the bat, worrying perhaps too much about his hands or feet, he sees a ball that looks ripe for the boundary and goes for the shot without that last second of concentration, looking to where he thinks the ball is travelling rather than ensuring that the bat is meeting the ball at the correct time and in the right place. One of the best times to check for this very simple fault is during the knock-up before a match – by the time the game has started it is a little too late! Use your knock-up or net to concentrate on watching that ball as closely as possible and a lot of the rest will follow quite naturally.

While you are at it, why not apply the same last-second concentration to your fielding and catching: see the ball right into your hands, which for catching should be held high and not around your waist. The lower your hands the greater the possibility that the ball will be out of your sight for a fraction of time, which is long enough for an error to be made. Oh, I know, you will see the brilliant catcher sometimes ignore this rule but the margin of error in catching is so small that it is wise to take every opportunity to improve the odds in your favour. And remember, the better player you become and the higher you move up the cricketing scale, the less time you will have to make your decision and the smaller will be the margin between success and failure.

Summed up, the two absolutely basic rules of batting are: (1) get in line with the ball, and (2) watch the ball on to the bat. Then you can begin to enjoy what Ranji called 'the most fascinating and delightful part of cricket'.

THE GRIP
AND THE STANCE

No one has yet bettered the oldest and simplest advice for gripping the bat: imagine you are picking up an axe. Lay the bat on the floor, face down, stand astride it and pick it up as if you were lifting an axe to chop wood. Then turn the hands round the handle in order to give yourself a correct cricketing stance and that grip should be proper and natural with the vees in your hands aligned in a position that will please your coach. Having said that I must add that one can be too dogmatic about the grip. It is an individual accommodation. Bodies are of different shapes and sizes, the sense of balance must vary and it comes down to a matter of adjusting the grip to suit yourself. The first book on cricket I ever read, and still read, is Sir Donald Bradman's *The Art of Cricket*, and I copied the grip, as a boy, from the illustration.

Boycott advises a grip around the middle of the handle, better nearer the top than the bottom (modern bats are balanced to be held in the middle) and emphasises the importance of making sure that your hands can close comfortably around the handle. He also points out that correct use of the left hand can cause strain 'especially for beginners'. To strengthen the left hand, try squeezing a squash ball as an exercise, even while reading a book or watching television.

It is interesting to note that an observation of Boycott's grip reveals that he, like Sir Leonard Hutton though to a lesser extent, tends to turn the left hand round so that the vee lines down the splice. It's a method I could not recommend, particularly for those learning, but it does give extra control and it does improve technique on difficult pitches. Both the great Yorkshiremen are renowned as 'bad wicket' batsmen. What you must remember is that the left hand is your control, the right hand provides the power. Above all, you must be comfortable but if being comfortable means that you are not connecting properly with the ball then something is wrong and you will need to re-examine your game. In the course of a career methods are sure to change but essentially one has to find one's own balance between comfort and efficacy.

Having gripped the bat you take your stance: the textbooks are pretty well in unison on this point: keep your feet about a foot apart, side-on, shoulders square, front elbow pointing forward, head facing straight down the wicket, eyes level. This is the classical stance, the perfect position from which you can move your feet into the right position at the right time. As the basis for teaching this is perfect advice. From that point onwards the variations begin as each player tries to make himself comfortable for his own way of playing. You must not allow yourself to feel cramped, you must always feel that you are standing alert but comfortable, loose and fluent, poised perfectly to address whatever problem the bowler or pitch may have for you.

No player is totally still as the bowler runs up. Everyone makes a small initial movement, forwards or back, to be in an anticipatory position. No one can afford to be caught static so, rather like a sprinter moving to the 'get set', everyone moves sufficiently to loosen himself without upsetting either the body balance or, most important, the line of vision. W. G. Grace insisted that the weight should be on the right foot. Modern advice (Boycott) suggests that the weight should be distributed evenly and that if the initial movement is off the back foot then it must be back and across. Never, never, move the back foot towards the leg-side; Ranji recalls that during his first two years of practice he had to have his right foot pegged down, a surprising but human confession from one of the greatest batsmen. Boycott prefers to bend the knees slightly, the bat being grounded just behind the right foot with the hands resting lightly on the left thigh: 'I move slightly back and across and it is absolutely vital that the head be kept perfectly still'.

My own stance has been criticised from time to time, but it is comfortable: a slight bend of the knees, relaxed, looking straight down the wicket, head and eyes completely still. Note how leading batsmen today take their stance. Graham Gooch didn't begin with his current stance. The bat is already half-lifted, the cause of some comment, but Graham clearly feels more comfortable with an earlier starting point and says that this position helps keep him side-on, his eyes level and better balanced. It certainly hasn't stopped him from scoring runs, and is a method now successfully adopted by others. Ian Botham has a totally relaxed, easy position, which illustrates what a perfectly natural player he is, with an inborn stance. Viv Richards, the greatest example today of a player whose colossal natural ability transcends all textbooks, does in fact start with a classical guard and stance. His variations, to the astonishment if not consternation of bowlers worldwide, begin when he starts to move from that position.

Although Viv often begins an innings by using a back and across movement the usual image one has of him is of that front foot coming across on to the off-stump, from where he has the ability to knock the bat through the leg-side, or to push off again on to the back foot if the ball is short. His Somerset colleague, Ian Botham, has a series of movements: first the back foot goes slightly back and across, then the front foot advances a little, leaving him with a broader stance immediately prior to receiving, still beautifully balanced to play off either front or back foot with equal power. In contrast to Botham, Allan Lamb tends to be looking to move forward, his front foot coming down the pitch a little but, note, he's always steady and ready to adapt. I prefer to get my back foot going first so that I do not feel rooted, how great the movement backward and across will be depends on circumstances. A guide to whether a player is on form and feeling good is to watch the timing of the initial movement. If it all happens naturally, in synchronisation with the turning of the bowler's arm, then the batsman is in 'good nick', as they say. If he is too early in his movement then he tends to become stuck, with the ball on the way and no time to worry about a second movement. If you are too late, well, that speaks for itself.

To sum up, know exactly what you are doing and do it at the right time, otherwise you are flirting with disaster. At the very highest level, facing a bowler who might be launching the ball at 90 mph plus, the calculation is that the batsman has only a split second to make

Gundappa Viswanath: Concentration, eye on the ball, moving into position.

Geoffrey Boycott: Forward defensive, killing the spin.

Martin Crowe: The off-drive.

The off-drive, almost straight.

Imran Khan: The on-drive.

Ian Botham: Lofted straight drive.

Clive Lloyd: The square drive.

Allan Border: Another square drive.

Barry Richards: Timing a cut.

Mohinder Amarnath: Dancing into the cut.

Vivian Richards: Late cutting.

The cut completed, the run called, the ball should be beating third man.

The pull, as seen by the keeper.

The pull, as seen by the bowler who wishes he hadn't.

A pull-drive, sometimes described as a 'lap-shot' for fairly obvious
reasons.

Gordon Greenidge: Hooking.

Mike Gatting: The sweep.

his decision so that to survive, never mind make runs, the preparatory move into position must be automatic, allowing him to make the necessary adjustments a split second later.

While on the subject of fast bowling, and thinking for a moment of those times when you will be forced to take evasive action, remember that although the textbook might advise you to be on the back foot initially, it is easier to duck if, once again, the weight is evenly balanced if not more on the front foot. This, I suppose, is an example of the batsman adapting to survive. Up to the turn of the century, or just before, according to W. G. Grace, the batsman played so much off the back foot that 'I can remember when batsmen regularly played the ball when it was only a few inches from their wickets'. The better preparation of pitches may have led to batsmen using the front foot more often, or playing the half-cock shot, 'playing the ball when it is level with the player's body'. That may sound old-fashioned but in some respects the Old Man can be very trendy. He may have advised resting the weight firmly on the back foot, but when it came to the pick-up he suggested lifting the bat so that the bottom of the blade was level with the stumps, another example of moving into position as early as possible.

As techniques and methods change through different eras, so does a batsman change during his career. That splendid coach and wonderful man Kenny Barrington would talk at length on how he had to change his stance on arrival in Australia, where he had to deal with the quicker bounce of a harder ball on firmer surfaces. He had to turn until he was slightly more square-on, which he felt put him in a better position to defend, or let the ball go. We are now venturing into the realms of the so-called 'two-eyed' stance. This is a misleading term which creates some confusion. As Boycott puts it, 'It is really a two-shouldered stance, useful for players who have difficulty in playing deliveries pitched on to their legs'. Geoffrey stresses how important it is to learn the correct stance first and to open the shoulders for tactical reasons only: 'the natural arc of the bat from a two-shouldered stance tends to be from inside to out, which is risky in itself'.

In recent times Peter Willey, a highly successful batsman with Northamptonshire, Leicestershire and England, has turned away from the traditional side-on address. Derek Randall, too, has turned more square-on. They say that they are more comfortable in their new position and I must add that we are talking about two very experienced batsmen who have performed well at the highest level and who may now feel that they can afford to follow the need to adapt. It is fair to say that with the technique and basic ability they already have at their command they can afford a few luxuries on style. The change of stance doesn't prevent either batsman from getting the left foot across at the right time and then giving the ball some mighty whacks. Peter Willey has always been capable of playing off the back foot to a full-length delivery just outside the off-stump, sending the ball right off the middle through extra cover at great speed, without his feet ever being in the textbook position.

Peter is able to hit the ball so hard and so accurately because his head would have been across, watching the bat meet the ball, even if he had left his feet behind. This is not to be recommended to the beginner: Peter is an exceptionally powerful player, and experienced enough to be able to balance his expertise, adding or subtracting to or from the technique required for each shot. The methods of Willey and Randall are perfectly illustrated by one of cricket's hoariest old stories about the farmer's lad who, recommended by a village club, arrives at the county nets as a complete unknown and sets about smashing the professional bowlers for many a mile. The county coach is horrified: 'You can't do that,' he says, 'you're doing it all wrong!'

In truth the art of good coaching is not to pontificate on what is right and wrong according to the textbook, but to have the ability to spot the natural, the player whose quickness and co-ordination of hand, eye and strength give him the confidence to play strokes without necessarily analysing what he is doing. He has to be encouraged and at the same time reminded of what is the accepted way of doing things, so that he has a basic drill to fall back on should things start to go wrong and his marvellous game start to fall apart.

I have had my own share of nightmares, and not only against the Hon T. M. Lamb at Northampton, where D. Gower lbw T. M. Lamb o was a scorebook entry eradicated only by the bowler's retirement to the administrative side of the game. Whether it be technique against pace, swing or turn, one is constantly learning and adjusting, especially when one comes up against the freaks of modern cricket, the likes of Garner at one end of the scale and Abdul Qadir at the other (I use the term freak with no disrespect to either gentleman). Every aspiring Test batsman has to guard himself, to cope with really hostile fast bowling, perhaps for the first time in his career. Grace believed he could tell when a fast ball was coming by a slight change in the bowler's run-up or action.

It helps if any indication of a variation in the next delivery can be noted and filed away in the mind. The very fastest bowlers are a breed all on their own and can demolish you, your theories, your technique and probably your stumps in three balls. All you have learned in the way of countering seam or swing or cut has to be hastily revised when you see Michael Holding beginning his run-up. You dare not let that dismay you. Very simply, you have to learn the techniques and then trust in your instinct and ability to play and make runs. You have to remember that there are batsmen who have played first-class cricket for many years, which means that they are successful, perhaps with much less natural ability than many other players. The difference is, to use a very hackneyed but apt word in this context, professionalism. The less gifted player has worked on his strengths, camouflaged his weaknesses, and applied himself and by dedication, concentration and using the products of a fiercely competitive nature, has won through to wear his county's colours and to face Holding, while the schoolboy they hailed as another Ted Dexter is still playing club cricket.

The secret is to make the most of your ability, to channel it in the right direction and play according to your limitations. Do not be frightened of being ridiculed if you discover some little mannerism helps reduce tension at the crease. Hobbs used to stand with the toe of his left foot in the air and just before the ball was delivered would tap the ground with his bat and return his foot to the natural position. Grace, according to Bradman, had a similar mannerism. Phil Mead would touch his cap to the umpire, pat the ground four times and take four little steps to his position before each ball, and Chris Tavaré goes on a little walkabout towards square leg between each ball.

Lastly, before we turn to playing the strokes, another thought from the Great Doctor: 'Sir Isaac Pitman used to say that after studying the rules and principles there were three great maxims to be taken to heart in learning shorthand. The first was practice, the second was practice and the third was practice'.

THE STROKES

Forward Defensive

Before we go on to discuss the very first and basic of all batting strokes, it might be interesting to discuss batting in general and the crucial importance of ensuring that each stroke is played correctly. As Bradman observed: 'A golfer may miss his drive, a tennis player his smash but one mistake by a batsman is usually his last'.

Bradman's two principal rules were (1) concentrate, and (2) watch the ball. Eyesight, obviously, is of great importance, but those with less than perfect vision should remember that at least two of the greatest contemporary batsmen, Clive Lloyd and Geoffrey Boycott, have always had to play wearing either glasses or contact lenses, though there is no doubt that some are blessed with better sight than others. A contemporary of Ranji's once said: 'Yes, I have keen eyesight. I could see the seam of the ball, but Ranji could see the stitches'. Bradman's success was so phenomenal that it was rumoured he had exceptional eyesight, and was thus able to see the ball earlier than most and react accordingly. Adelaide University became interested in this claim and asked Bradman to submit to some tests which proved that his reactions were, in fact, slightly slower than those of the average university student. Bradman certainly believed that it was in watching the ball leave the bowler's hand that he first had a clue as to the bowler's intentions.

Ranji made some very pertinent comments on stroke play in general: 'An absolute beginner, when a bat is first put into his hands, follows the promptings of nature. Almost every stroke he attempts is some form of pull with a cross bat'. Having emphasised the importance of building on a correct technique, Ranji then adds, characteristically, 'A stroke which is safe and effective cannot be bad in cricket'. Ranji's philosophy of batting is then summarised. 'Just as there should always be a latent aggressive element in back play, so there should be a latent defensive in all forward play . . .' But: 'Even defensive strokes should be played in such a manner as to contain latent scoring power . . . The only parallel I can think of in this respect is a move at chess: when your opponent attacks with a certain move and you counteract with a move of your own, your aim should always be that your own move be not only defensive but have an attacking force of its own'.

Dr Grace favours a more cautious, English approach: 'Cultivate patience in the early stages of your innings and get accustomed to the bowling before you take any liberties. The impatient desire for fast scoring engenders recklessness. There is an old maxim which I recommend viz: Take care of your stumps and the runs will take care of themselves'. So the stroke that is the very essence of the Doctor's 'cultivating patience' is the forward defensive. A classic illustration was Colin Cowdrey, watched from square-on, his front leg slightly bent, but perfectly straight down the pitch; you could see the profile of the bat, angled to the ground next door to the pad, giving no way through to the ball; the head, feet and hands were all in line with the face of the bat to the line of the ball. This is the very basis of the stroke. Of course, there are variations: the bat is angled for various bowlers, particularly against spinners, against whom this stroke is mostly used. It is the main defence against less than quick bowling of a full-length or just short of a full-length ball.

The very good players of spin like to improvise. Facing a top-class spinner is a test of skill, reflexes and intelligence, and the duel becomes almost personal, between two artists. Keith Fletcher, for instance, likes to close the face of the bat a little, putting a squeeze on the ball, killing the spin between bat and pad. Other batsmen may open the face – depending on which way the ball is spinning – to let the ball run off. But beware, if the ball is spinning away, presenting less of the face of the bat needs experience, control and confidence if you are not to give the slips an edge. Tactics may be dependent upon the positioning of the close field. Modern captains like to set a short square leg and a silly point for the spinners and when these two men, padded and helmeted, are in position, a top-class bowler who can keep his line and length while spinning the ball presents many problems.

It is then that the ancient principle of playing with the bat alongside the pad can be dangerous with two men placed to take the ball that 'pops' or even scoop it off the bat. To counter this peril some batsmen have taken to thrusting the leg down the pitch and playing with the bat behind the pad. Many bowlers will maintain that this is not a proper shot and that the batsman would therefore be open to an appeal to leg-before. The batsman argues that he is producing a perfectly legitimate defensive stroke to protect his stumps. A variation is to play with the bat well advanced in front of the pad, a technique I have never really favoured myself but which I have watched Jack Birkenshaw, no mean player of spinners, use very successfully during my early years at Leicestershire.

Boycott is a master of the forward defensive, having played it more often than most. Joking apart, Geoffrey is such a fine technician that his method in any shot is always an excellent example for any young player. His forward defensive says to the whole world 'They shall not pass'; the head, the bat, the pad are all in the right place, covering the ball, reducing to a minimum any gap through which the ball might pass, and then, finally, he drops the ball dead, taking all the rigidity out of the bat, allowing the ball to hit the full face and to spend all its venom on a smooth, slightly yielding wooden wall. Geoffrey points out, very wisely, that 'there is no sense in playing at a ball that can be left alone; play decisively or leave strictly alone; do not fence at deliveries outside the off-stump'. Sometimes easier said than done!

Backward Defensive

Expertise in back defensive play, says Bradman, is vital: 'Master it at all costs if you have ambitions'. Ted Dexter, playing the stroke against Wesley Hall in the early 1960s, immediately springs to mind as an ideal illustration. The backward defensive is played to the shorter, straight ball; any delivery wide is open to attack or to be left alone. Basically this is to be played against the quickest bowling, a side-on shot, elbow high, bat facing down the pitch. The pace and bounce will decide how high the shot has to be played. The movement should be simple and straightforward: standing still you see that the ball is on the line of the stumps but pitching short; move your back foot across, get into line, lift the bat high and play the ball down. That, theoretically, is how it's done, but when you are facing really fast bowlers there are any number of improvisations.

The player starts to move across and on to the back foot early in his preparation and may not always be in the classical Dexter position. For a split second you may achieve the correct position as the ball arrives, but your momentum soon takes you into a different position, not to be condemned if your balance is maintained. The movement may not look stylish and will certainly displease the purists but the principal concern on these occasions is to play the ball down safely, with perhaps a modicum of self-defence involved! Gone, sadly, are the days when W. G. could growl: 'I don't like defensive strokes – you only get three off 'em'. Even Bradman has to concede: 'You cannot attack every ball'.

With the predominance of fast bowling in modern first-class cricket, judgement of and reaction to short-pitched bowling is essential and, especially early in one's innings, defence needs to be well organised. This is basically either a question of getting over the ball and playing it down, or of removing gloves, head, body and everything else out of the line of the ball, with the idea of letting it safely and harmlessly by!

Now and again the likes of Marshall, Garner, Imran and company are going to produce unplayable deliveries and extract that extra unexpected bounce, and it naturally takes a certain speed of reaction, allied to good technique, to counter such deliveries. If one can remove everything out of the line of the ball, whether by swaying or ducking, so much the better, but as ever the golden rule applies: keep your eye on the ball; it is sometimes amazing how much time there is to make minor adjustments, even in a split second.

The Cricketer magazine, concerned at the amount of head-high bowling in Test matches, particularly when the West Indies are playing, made an interesting suggestion that the Laws should be amended, making a catch legal only from the bat and not, as at present, also from the gloves and handle. I do not think it takes too much consideration to dismiss that sort of suggestion, however tempted one might be as a batsman to make life easier for oneself! As we have seen, there are ways and means of avoiding or playing the short-pitched ball and of turning it to the batsman's advantage. Part of the technique of playing fast bowling is developing the ability to drop the wrists so that you can ride the ball. Of course you have to be quick, you have to be fit and your reactions must be first-class but we are talking, by and large, of Test cricket, the highest level of the game.

While every batsman agrees with efforts to curtail the frequency of the bouncer I have still to be convinced that this can be done through legislation. Some illustrious figures in cricket have proposed and supported the drawing of a line across the pitch beyond which a bowler would have to pitch to avoid being no-balled. The difficulty would be agreeing on a distance that would apply to all fast bowlers. You could hardly draw a different line for each bowler. A further suggestion is that the umpires should decide on where to draw the line. But how can they make a judgement until they have seen the bowlers in action and how can they forecast the behaviour of a three-day or a five-day pitch from day to day or even from session to session? Whatever good intentions there may be, one has to accept that such schemes leave a lot to be desired, especially from the bowler's point of view.

Law 42 mentions intimidation. I am sure that due consideration was given to that word before it was incorporated into law and yet it does seem to me to reflect on the courage of the batsman. No one likes to admit they are being intimidated, whether it be when walking through a picket line or facing Malcolm Marshall. This contentious matter has been with first-class cricket almost since the dawn of history. Fortunately it is rarely a controversy at school and club level where I can commend Bradman's advice: 'I like to feel when playing back defensively that I was hitting the ball either towards the bowler or to the on-side rather than towards cover. It gave me a feeling of security that I was, if anything, coming from outside the line of flight and therefore guarding against a possible slip catch from the ball that went away. It is so much easier to follow the ball that goes towards the leg-side'. Bradman is constantly advising the batsman to move in that direction: 'Footwork, generally, should be constantly taking the batsman towards the off'.

Driving

(a) To the off-side
Driving, says Geoffrey Boycott, 'is the most satisfying stroke in the game, a long, smooth swing that takes the bat through the ball rather than to the ball. It is important that the right hand, giving steadiness and

extra power, does not come into the shot too soon'.

The off-drive is played to a full-length ball outside the off-stump, one of the shots in which it is essential to move your feet to get to the pitch of the ball; if your head is not in line you are liable to make that little error (especially as you are trying to hit the ball harder) and take your eye off the ball at the last moment. It's rather like trying to hit a golf ball too hard. Many, including professionals, aim to smash the ball out of sight and either take their eye away or lift their head at the last moment. To play the off-drive perfectly the weight should be forward, the body balanced, the head forward, and the arm in line with the ball; the bat goes through the line with the follow-through hands high, finishing over the shoulder, Hutton-style, or with the bat and hands high without breaking the wrists, like Allan Lamb.

If you are in position quickly and correctly all that is then needed is to time the shot; if you try to hit too hard you will find that your weight will go back a little, and your head with it, and that when bat meets ball it will not have your full weight behind it. Your whole stroke will be bat speed on the ball, which can fly anywhere. Timing is the key and timing is making sure that your weight is in the right place.

These principles remain valid if you play, against the quicker bowlers normally, the off-drive off the back foot. The ball will travel more towards square, cover to extra cover, but the movement into position is similar, the weight resting on the back foot. Extra caution is needed because the bowler has a fraction more time in which to make the ball leave the bat, so that it is even more important to be in line and to watch the ball on to the bat in order to detect and counter any late movement.

Back-foot driving can be one of the most exciting strokes in cricket – it is particularly Caribbean in flavour, no doubt thanks to the consistency in pace of both their wickets and their bowlers!

(b) On-drive

This is played to the ball that is pitched in the area of middle- and leg-stump; again the front foot should be just inside the line of the ball but opened a little so that the bat has room to swing straight through and the straighter you play the better. There is a tendency to try to 'work' the ball; many modern players are 'workers'. As they play the ball they turn the bat and thus tend to aim the ball more towards mid-wicket than mid-on. But beware: there is a danger that if the ball turns away off the pitch, or swings away, you may give the bowler a return catch as the ball takes the leading edge. It is also very possible, as a few famous players have discovered to their great embarrassment, to play round a straight ball. More than a few batsmen have been out leg-before or bowled as a result.

Keith Fletcher 'works' the ball very well, putting it away very smartly when the opportunity occurs, and he is also very adept at keeping the ball on the ground thanks to the position of his arms and hands, which makes sure the ball is not scooped or flicked into the air. His Essex colleague Graham Gooch is another very strong through mid-on and mid-wicket though he tends to come straighter through the ball (no bad thing) and uses that high back lift to provide a long, free swing at the ball.

The straight drive is played to the ball pitched on middle-stump, or between middle-and off-stump, with all the same principles applied. Bradman makes the very good point that while the drive is employed mostly against the medium to quick bowlers, from the crease 'against a slow bowler a batsman may, by fast footwork and good judgement, essay out of his crease to make a half-volley out of a ball which otherwise would have been of good length. In this way he can make punishing drives and upset the bowler's control'.

The natural and exciting extension of the standard straight drive is the lofted version. The ball has to be hit on the up as it is almost impossible to lift a half-volley; again the bat must swing through the line. The tendency is to leave the crease to play the shot, to catch the ball on the up, but it can be played from within the crease, two models to watch again being Richards and Botham. It is a stroke that should be attempted only when you are well set and confident because there is always a large element of risk. Aiming the ball into the air carries all the attendant dangers of the mis-hit. The ball has to be middled and it has to be struck with power and to be directed away from the field.

One-day cricket has undoubtedly revised the lofted drive and those expert and capable enough will use it in first-class cricket, often as a tactical means of breaking up the close field in order to be able to progress with much less risky singles and twos. Viv Richards showed us a lot of the lofted drive towards the end of his magnificent Texaco Cup innings against England at Old Trafford in 1984. Stepping back to the quick bowlers, he found a less orthodox means of making room for the bat to swing and at the same time made it increasingly difficult for the bowlers who, of course, were aiming at the blockhole, trying to pin him down with yorkers. Ian Botham, of course, has no fears of lofting the ball – how can one forget his hitting McDermott straight back into the pavilion at Edgbaston from his first ball? However, despite having the talent to do this to quicker bowlers, it is to the spinners that Ian will take this form of attack most often and most effectively; with one of the fullest swings of a cricket bat one will ever see.

Perhaps Grace used similar tactics against quicker bowlers in his day because Ranji records: 'It is said of the Doctor that no one can bowl him a yorker'. Bradman, whether driving on the ground or in the air, was clearly a ferocious opponent. After advising against driving against the swing, which is common sense, he adds: 'Just because a ball swings it doesn't mean it cannot be driven. There is nothing better than a mildly-curving, out-swinging half-volley to drive through the covers. The swing helps it like a charm'. Every shot he played he played with thought: 'I would often deliberately play a ball to a certain position just to keep the fielder there. I didn't want him shifted to a position which would have saved four instead of one'.

Cutting

The cut is an aggressive shot with which to attack medium and fast bowling outside the off-stump and as such is a very valuable source of runs. You have to be confident of the bounce of the ball in order to play the shot successfully: again the basics are to get the back foot across, transfer the weight and then hit down on the ball. Here I feel I should differentiate between the cut and the flash, the latter description having been successfully adopted by the media in recent years. The flash is played when the back foot is not quite far enough across and the ball meets – or misses – the ball at the wrong angle. The stroke is then no longer controlled and there is a good possibility of your being caught in the gulley cover area.

Ranji, after praising the way Grace cut the ball, 'from his shoulders', went on to say: 'The late cut is the most telling, the square cut is the safest. The forward cut (square-drive) I do not care for as a stroke, though it is very brilliant when properly executed, the sooner the cut is made the squarer the ball will travel'. Boycott's analytical mind spells out the dangers: 'Width and length are important. If the delivery is not that wide use the back foot forcing shot. For the late cut let the ball pass your body. It is a stroke most often used on firm surfaces and it is sometimes better to omit the late cut on a slow pitch'.

The square-drive and the square cut propel the ball into roughly the same area but are very different shots in their execution. The square-drive can be a profitable shot but needs care. For the cut the bat is held horizontally and the wrists rolled at the moment of contact: for the drive the bat inclines towards the vertical, is open-faced and, as with all driving, room must be found to swing the bat.

A variation on the cut is to take a wider ball on the up and cut it over the close field, an especially rewarding shot when the ball is bouncing and the bowler is having difficulty with his line. Gordon Greenidge, for one, has broken a few hearts with this shot. Peter Willey can be a savage cutter. I will always remember him in Antigua cutting Colin Croft savagely square for six. I can also remember helping a short ball from Michael Holding over the third man boundary – a treasured memory of something which is unlikely to be repeated in a hurry!

The late cut is really a delayed square cut, used best perhaps against the ball spinning away from the bat. You will see, occasionally, a top-class batsman, well set, who will break almost every rule in the book. One rule he ignores at his extreme peril is to try to cut the ball turning in to the batsman. Another temptation when playing the late cut is to indulge in the extra time allowed while the spinner turns the ball away outside the off-stump and to take the eye off the ball – don't. There can always be a slight variation in the bounce or the amount of turn so it really does become even more necessary to follow the ball right on to the bat. If you do lose concentration for an instant there is every possibility that you offer a faint edge to the keeper, a familiar sight. The difference is minimal; we are talking about a yard in terms of concentration.

In his day Bradman was worried that the late cut might disappear from the repertoire, so much was the bowling concentrated on the leg-stump. However 'completely by accident the best shot I ever played was a late cut', he says. 'In the Leeds Test of 1930 I jumped down the pitch to drive but found I had misjudged the flight of the ball. When trying to get back I slipped and fell. However, by retaining my balance and control, I managed to back cut the ball to third man for a single'. There is a photograph of that famous incident (Central Press) which shows Bradman on his knees watching the ball scoot past a surprised George Duckworth and a motionless first slip.

This was the innings in which Bradman scored, at the age of 21 years and 318 days, 105 before lunch, 115 between lunch and tea and 89 in the final session for a then world record of 334. His 200 came in 214 minutes. The England attack included Larwood, Maurice Tate, Geary and Dick Tyldesley.

The Back-Foot Force

This is a stroke played to the ball short of a length on or just outside the off-stump. The back foot, head and body are taken back and across, the bat comes down straight and the ball is aimed between cover and mid-off. The stroke can also be played on the leg-side provided that the foot gets inside the line of the ball to give the bat room to swing, aiming towards mid-on and mid-wicket – the straighter the attempt to play the ball the better. Again, the model is Viv Richards, even more than brilliant with his on-side play.

Bradman makes the telling point that the back-foot force through mid-on is especially effective in that it is difficult territory for the bowler, who will be trying to keep his balance. If wide mid-on is pulled into a straighter position to block the shot there is often an inviting gap between mid-wicket and mid-on. He mentions a particularly disconcerting stroke of Compton's whereby the great man would back away down the leg-side to force the slow left-hander or leg-spinner through the covers. Bradman's somewhat sardonic comment is: 'If you can do it and get away with it well and good, but I don't recommend you to try unless your place in the team is already secure'.

The Pull

This is one of the most spectacular shots in cricket, played with the bat horizontal and to the shorter ball. Again you must get back and across, holding the bat high, bringing it down on to the ball and rolling the wrists. The ball must be waist- or stomach-high and short enough to give you time to play the shot.

Bradman, by all accounts, was a ferocious practitioner of this stroke. He was, he says, 'compelled by circumstances to play most of my cricket on concrete pitches covered with coir matting. As anyone with experience on them knows these pitches give rise to a more uniform but much higher bounce than turf. I was very short and consequently found great difficulty in playing with a straight bat but the ball pitched short of a length on the stumps. It came too high for comfort. Remember, I was a schoolboy and often faced the bowling of grown men. To overcome this predicament I developed the pull shot to a marked degree'.

Control is the key word in playing the pull: you must get on top of the ball otherwise it can fly anywhere. The destination of the ball will depend upon where it pitches. A normal pull shot should see the ball ending somewhere backward of square of the leg-side. As you become more proficient with the shot and more efficient in its execution it should be possible to drag it through mid-wicket from outside the off-stump. Note Bradman's point about the uniform bounce on concrete pitches. Turf is far less predictable and the pull should be used very sparingly unless you are certain of the height of the bounce. So if you do have confidence in the bounce and the ball is short the pull becomes a valuable weapon, particularly if you are dealing with a close-set field on the leg-side, to an off-spinner or a medium pace bowler. Played properly the shot involves a pivot so that it is essential to keep your feet apart to preserve your balance and you should end up facing roughly in the square-leg direction.

The Hook

The hook is not to be confused with the pull, as often happens. The hook is played to the ball that is dug in, pitching on an even shorter length, reaching the batsman chest-high or above and a ball that is therefore that much harder to control as you need to get the bat that much higher to bring the ball under control. Fleet footwork is essential to play the hook properly: you must move quickly inside the line of the ball as you move backward and across and then, watching the ball all the way, you aim to roll the wrists again to bring the ball down and under control. Watch Viv Richards play the hook; look out for Ian Chappell on film because he could hook superbly.

Never forget that this is a dangerous shot and not just to your wicket. Geoff Boycott, stressing the importance of getting your feet into the correct position, records that he was 11 years old when he attempted a hook and ended up in hospital. He had four stitches in a gash over his right eye and still carries the scar. Many famous players have been in trouble when a hook shot has gone wrong. Even Bradman had his problems: Bill Bowes once knocked his cap sideways on the old Bramall Lane pitch and the great man warns against playing hooks and pulls on a greasy English pitch, much rarer now than they were in his day: 'If you do, have a spare set of teeth ready'.

The difficulty with the hook is that it is so hard to control the move as bowler and pitch get quicker. On those occasions it is virtually impossible to keep the ball down and it needs only the slightest error of timing to drop the ball down the throat of long-leg, posted there for that very purpose. It's wise to check your boundary distances and the positioning of the field before you indulge yourself in what is one of cricket's most exciting strokes. If you are playing well the hook is always a temptation – no one can deny a certain pleasure when everything clicks, you meet the ball perfectly and it disappears miles away for six. This elation is quite easily tempered by those occasions when you do everything nearly right but find the ball has only nestled nicely in deep square-leg's hands.

Perhaps one could say that the time to use the hook is when the opposing bowler is not really fast, but thinks he is, and when he is bowling on a slow pitch. Then, when the ball is dug in it will sit up and beg to be hit, and the batsman has all the time necessary to play the shot properly to place the ball where he chooses.

If you are at all unhappy with your execution of the hook shot then my advice would be: don't play it. When the bowler pitches short you will have to learn how to duck and sway which, done successfully, can be more discouraging to the bowler than actually attacking him. If he knows that you are prepared to hook him then he does have the option of putting two men back and bowling in the hope that you might make an error that would put up a catch almost anywhere on the leg-side, square or behind. But if you ignore his shorter ball (Reg Simpson is remembered as a master of evasion) then you commit the bowler to a growing feeling of frustration, a loss of temper and control, or a change of tactics, which must work to your advantage.

The Glance

The glance is played to a ball of full-length on or just outside leg-stump. Let the ball come to you and then glide it down to long-leg. A gentle turn of the bat should suffice. There is an alternative shot to be played to a delivery in this position, when you aim to play the ball hard and square off the wicket, what we know as the 'pick-up' shot. It is somewhere between a glance and a wide on-drive: let the ball come to you, open up the body and as the ball swings across just turn the wrists a little, then finish square or just behind square.

It is a stroke that is very much dependent upon timing. Graham Gooch and Keith Fletcher are the models to watch. Be very careful to get the hands in the right place because if you don't get the bat over the ball you may find yourself giving a fairly straightforward catch. At the same time there is scope for the six-hit: if a proper connection is made on the pick-ups the ball will fly out of the ground. Ranji was a recognised master in this area and points out that on a hot and tiring day the glance can be both very profitable and sparing of effort. He is also remembered for one very individual shot, a glance off the back foot played to a ball on his stumps! 'It is a very useful stroke', wrote the Prince, 'when bowlers are trying to bowl maidens.'

He then recalled a match between Somerset and Sussex in 1896, Somerset needing slightly more than 200 to win in the fourth innings: 'The wicket was rather crumbly. Six wickets fell for 23. But Mr Palairet at the end of the game was not out 83. He managed to secure the bowling over after over thanks to a judicious use of this back forcing stroke'.

Ranji moved his left foot across the stumps towards point, faced the ball with his body from the waist upwards, watched the ball on to the bat and then despatched it at the last moment with a quick turn of the wrist. 'The great thing is to have the bat from the start in the line of the ball so that in the case of a mistake in timing the ball hits the bat and not the leg', he said. 'It is always a risky thing to play straight balls with any part of the person in front of the wicket; but so long as the bat is in the right place there is no fear of getting out leg before.'

I certainly agree with him in terms of the risk – generally one plays the straight ball back whence it came, and glancing is really a means of making contact with a ball already sliding down the leg-side.

The Sweep

The sweep is one of those shots that tend to be forbidden by the more orthodox-minded. It is also a good attacking variation against the spinner. You must be sure of the line of the ball because more and more umpires are prepared to give a batsman out if he sweeps and misses a straight ball. The other fundamental rule in playing the sweep is to keep the ball down; if you do get a top edge there is a danger of being caught down the leg-side, deep or close-in.

Remember, it is always a risky shot, even if you play it

well. So many things can go wrong, not least in that the bounce of the ball may deceive you: with the sweep the margin of error need be no more than an inch. I play the sweep less now than at the start of my career, perhaps because I am now a better judge of just when it is feasible to play the shot. I have been bowled, comprehensively, when playing the sweep and when I have got just about everything wrong. Another attendant risk is to play the sweep out of desperation: a bowler has been pinning you down, accurate and straight, in a limited-overs match and you look to try something different to keep the score moving.

As for an example of how to play the sweep I can recommend Mike Gatting who destroyed the Indian spinners throughout the 1984–85 tour. Ian Botham also plays it well although Ian has a tendency to sweep the ball out of the ground rather than settling for the controlled version all along the ground. He gives it such a whack that the shot becomes less of a sweep and more of another special edition from the unique Botham catalogue. He removes any risk of top-edging by hitting the ball so hard it will clear any boundary; simple enough if you are Ian Botham. Two further excellent sweepers are Graham Gooch and Alan Knott, that master of improvisation. We have touched on the reverse sweep in the section devoted to extraordinary shots: again, a very useful and surprising weapon in the armoury provided it is played properly. Derek Pringle plays it as well as anyone, Ian Botham wins a lot of publicity when he fails with it (he also succeeds) and I haven't a clue how to do it. I have tried but the results have been disastrous.

VARIATIONS ON
A THEME

Not one of these strokes can be said to be totally justified in that they all carry an inordinate amount of risk. Fortunately cricket isn't always played by insurance assessors. The great batsmen, like great artists, have always wanted to improvise and entertain as well as to accumulate runs.

The Reverse Sweep

The reverse sweep is one such stroke, normally played in one-day cricket and against spinners. It is automatically linked with Ian Botham but other regular exponents include Mike Gatting and Derek Pringle, among those who actually get it mostly right. Mushtaq Mohammed, of Northamptonshire and Pakistan, is the man usually credited with introducing it – or re-introducing it – to cricket in England although I have no doubt that it has been played on and off for a century or more.

Timing, and the angle of the bat, are absolutely crucial. Make the slightest error in judgement and there's an excellent chance of finding a top edge and either giving a fielder an easy catch, or, of course, having to replace a couple of teeth. Furthermore, if you pick the wrong ball for this stroke and miss it, then it can be a more embarrassing walk than usual back to the pavilion.

The Draw or Chinese Cut

Not the same but similar in execution. The draw was a legitimate stroke of the Golden Age and Ranji regretted its passing: 'Nowadays most batsmen play forward or adopt the "half-cock" stroke, which means playing the ball when it is level with the batsman's body. Owing to this new style of play the old "draw", which used to be a very favourite stroke, has entirely gone out. Tom Hearne used to play this stroke very skilfully and to score from it very freely'.

The essence of the shot is to turn, with a very quick flick of the wrists, a ball overpitched on the leg-side through your own legs to, you hope, the utter consternation of the wicket-keeper and close field. To me, this seems so unlikely to happen that in modern times, though the shot can often be seen, if the batsman tells you he played it deliberately he is almost certainly a liar. It is now better known as the Chinese or Harrow Cut.

Waving or Fishing

Often used to describe batsmen who have failed to play a forcing shot off the back foot or failed to cut correctly, and have consequently been caught by the wicket-keeper or missed by a mile. A term gleefully adopted by county cricketers.

The Walleroo

Glorious title for the upward cut, as exemplified by Derek Randall or Peter Willey, when the ball is propelled over point at a fearsome rate of knots.

The Pull-drive

An up-market version of the slog, exemplified by Derek Randall, always a masterly exponent of the art of improvisation (the fact that he watches the ball like a hawk is, of course, vital to this). It is the shot with which he can destroy the best of spinners, whichever way the ball is turning, for instance the likes of Abdul Qadir, even though the latter might have won such a battle once or twice as well. The shot is certainly an effective method of exasperating sensitive bowlers.

The Slog

The oldest shot in cricket, the most natural for novices of all ages to attempt. Aimed at the mid-wicket boundary it is often accompanied by lifting heads and tumbling bails. The term is also used to describe virtually any stroke that smacks of frustration on the batsman's part, whether effectively completed or not.

PART II

'Deliberate Speed, Majestic Instancy'

Francis Thompson

PACE BOWLERS

Dennis Lillee has to be at the top; like a man who has climbed Everest his figures alone put him there, a fast bowler who has taken 355 Test wickets and ten or more in a Test match seven times. While I was still learning the game I saw Lillee, on television, at his 'fiery colt' stage, fast but raw and wayward. He learned to assert control so quickly that it was obvious even to my young eye that here was a quick bowler who could rattle Australia's opponents for many years. In 1974–75, with Thommo at the other end, it was painful to watch England's batsmen under such pressure. I don't suppose I was the only young Englishman who was pleased that I wasn't playing in my first overseas series!

Lillee then developed into one of the truly great fast bowlers; indeed it could be argued that he is the greatest, judging as best we can from records, films and historical accounts of his rivals. If I were to propose Dennis Lillee as the greatest fast bowler of all time I fancy that Geoffrey Boycott would be quick to second the motion. Even in 1982–83, when he played in only a couple of Tests and then returned to the Australian side for the one-day series, he remained a formidable opponent, retaining still that beautiful action, the control, the exact length, the odd ball darting away, a marvellous visual lesson for any aspiring bowler. Dennis Lillee is one of the bowlers who can make any batsman tingle as that batsman walks out to take guard. You know that almost every ball will be a test of your skill and with every score there will be an extra sense of exhilaration. It's never boring.

Batting against Lillee has been one of the most enjoyable experiences of my career, even when he has won the day. He was always quick, bowled some very useful and unexpected bouncers and most deliveries would seam or swing a little. I accept that I never played against him when he was at his absolute peak as a fast bowler – for which I have to be grateful – but I would contend that I did have to face him in the years when he was a better overall bowler, if not quite as sharp.

He was the fast bowler every captain wanted because Dennis was not only a superb technician, a professional to his fingertips, but he also thought for himself; he always knew what he was doing and adjusted his game according to the needs of the moment. Having a fully-fit Lillee in the team must have allowed a half-dozen Australian captains to sleep easily at night. However, Dennis became such a strong and powerful figure in the Australian team that at least one captain, Kim Hughes, had a few arguments with him. How he got on with Ian and Greg Chappell I cannot say, but a player's status and authority in the dressing-room must change according to his length of occupation.

Dennis also exploded the myth of 'thick' Australian fast bowlers. He is a very intelligent man, especially when it comes to working out how to dismiss his leading opponents. He hated Derek Randall or, to put it more precisely, he hated bowling at him. You could always

Richard Ellison: Swing is king.

Les Taylor: Tireless, accurate, underestimated.

Craig McDermott: Tiger, tiger, learning fast.

Philippe Edmonds: Theoretician.

Abdul Qadir: Pick this one if you can.

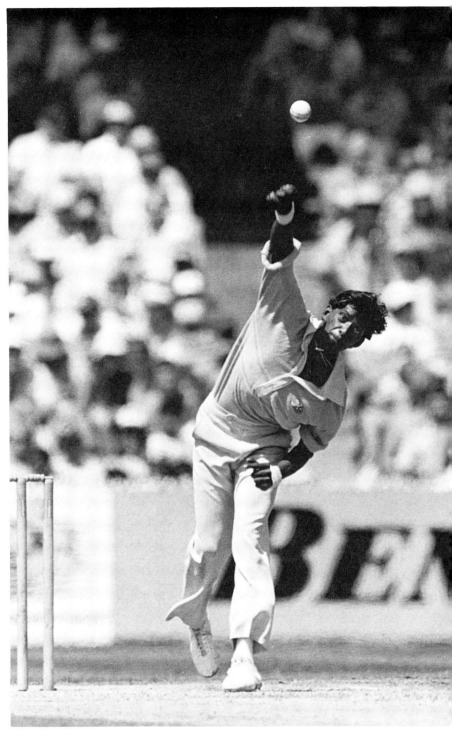

Sivaramakrishnan: Moody.

Roger Harper: The man with the longer arm.

Eden Gardens, Calcutta – one of the world's great cricket grounds.

Sunil Gavaskar: A powerful cover drive.

Paul Downton: Natural talent, high ability.

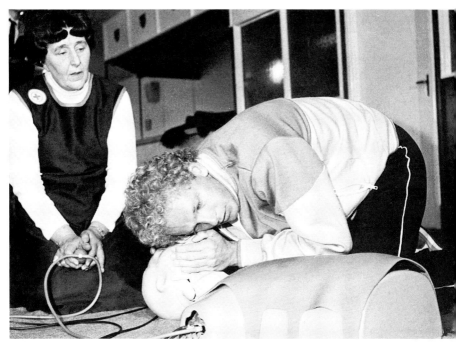

'Can he manage another burst from the top end?' Actually I'm undertaking respiratory training from the Red Cross.

Vice captain Peter Willey and the Benson and Hedges Cup, captured by the Running Fox.

With A.R.B. – good friend, good bloke, great player.

The straight drive towards 215, Fifth Test, Edgbaston, 1985.

The secret is to let 'Both' do it his own way.

England: All the bright company, 1985.

England: It was a good vintage.

guarantee that the arrival of 'Arkle' at the crease would fire Dennis even more. I'm still not sure, well as I know Derek, whether his antics when taking guard and preparing to receive the ball were calculated or merely an expression of his nervous energy: whatever they were, they enraged Lillee and, among other Australians, Rodney Hogg.

Lillee and Thomson go together like Larwood and Voce or Trueman and Statham. Before Thommo injured his shoulder he was, by common consent among all the players of my generation and the one preceding us, the quickest. His peculiar, slinging action gave him the ability to win bounce, sudden unsuspected bounce, from the most dead of pitches. Even after the shoulder treatment, which necessitated an adjustment that prevented him from bowling flat out for long spells, he was still capable of surprising even top players with a sudden thunderbolt. Clive Lloyd once told me of an occasion when Thommo had been brought back into the team against West Indies. Clive and his partner thought they had just about taken control of the game and were starting to put the pressure on Australia's bowlers when Thommo, apparently tired, suddenly produced a ball which smacked Clive on the jaw − a lesson for every batsman to bear in mind when he thinks things are starting to go his way!

Jeff Thomson was portrayed through that 1974–75 series, at least according to my memory, as a mean and nasty man. The implication was that he and Lillee deliberately fired extra fast deliveries at the batsman's heart, ball after ball; in other words, murderous bowling. I don't accept that although I admit I didn't play against them on that tour. It is the fast bowler's job to unsettle a batsman. He has to aim at something and the area of the chest is not a bad target, if you are fast enough and can generate enough bounce to get the ball that high. After all, it's up to the batsman to defend himself and there is no limit to the amount of body padding allowed. I do resent the suggestion that any of the Aussies was a mean and nasty man. Off the field Thommo is a lovely guy; he is relaxed, loves his swimming and his fishing, and has the great capacity – and this is what made him a great bowler – to get fired up once on the field. Ian Wooldridge's creation 'Terror Tompkins' is a great character and gives us all a good laugh but I can assure you he bears little resemblance to the Jeff Thomson I know.

Geoff Lawson is a very fiery character on the field and works very hard for Australia's cause. Always an aggressive bowler, he has won respect around the world through his ability to come back (always the sign of a top-class bowler) when you feel he must be exhausted, and then whip out two or three batsmen. He can be genuinely quick and he has carried Australia's attack on many occasions over the last few years. In the winter of 1984 Clive Lloyd praised 'Henry' Lawson as the world's number one white fast bowler and not too many of us would have quarrelled with that judgement. A fairly quiet man off the field, he doesn't say a great deal and seems to take refuge in his image of the professional man. A qualified optometrist (he deals with spectacles, contact lenses etc.), Geoff will also be remembered for his superb outfielding. He's fast, clean in the pick-up, long and accurate in the throw and has taken some marvellous catches. Channel 9 should have enough material depicting Lawson's outfielding to make an excellent demonstration film. Geoff has also been a useful eight or nine in any Test batting order. He doesn't give his wicket away and can play to order, he can stick it out or he can hit out. We and the West Indies have suffered a few times playing against him.

Rodney Hogg won't be remembered as one of Australia's great fast bowlers but he will get a mention in any book of mine, not least for his tremendous performance in 1978–79 when he took 41 England wickets for a team that lost the series 5–1. That says a lot for the man. In short spells Hoggy could be as quick as any of them. He was unpredictable but he did have that little bit extra, on his day, that marks and qualifies a class fast bowler. All Test fast bowlers will put you on the back foot and make the ball move; some will give you more loose deliveries than others and the very good or great ones will have that bit extra, that extra bounce, extra pace, extra movement that will get the good player out if he fails to make the correct re-adjustment in the last second left to him in which to make the appropriate counter-move. If that happens and you are out, when you analyse the incident afterwards you have to say to yourself, at least, 'Well, there was nothing I could have done about that. He was simply too good for me. But I'll know what to look out for next time'.

Craig McDermott almost literally burst on the world cricket scene within 12 months, and soon picked up the nickname 'The Tiger'. He began against the West Indies – at least it was downhill after that – and dismissed Vivian Richards, obviously making an impact. Before the Australians arrived in England in 1985 I sought out my old friend Brian Davison who had been playing for Tasmania, in part to seek an update on the activities of Mr McDermott. I respect Davo's opinion and he was full of praise for a young fast bowler with heart and aggression who was clearly a long, long way from his full potential. All Davo's predictions about McDermott were borne out in that rainy summer of 1985, when he rarely found a pitch to suit himself.

Overall on that tour McDermott could have been accused of inconsistency. He sometimes struggled to find his line and length but when he did marshal all his resources and put his game together, as he did at Old Trafford when he took eight England wickets on what could never be called a fast bowler's pitch, he gave us an indication of what he might achieve for Australia in the future. He did a lot of hard work into the breeze at the start, while Lawson had the wind behind him, and when he was switched to gain the advantage he bowled straight and quickly, confirming his strength and stamina, and his wickets were a justified reward for a splendid effort.

Of the West Indians' whole gallery of great fast bowlers in my time Andy Roberts impressed me as the most knowledgeable and thoughtful of them all. He knew a great deal about opposing batsmen, and he also knew when to bowl, that is when his bowling would have the maximum impact. When Andy did begin to lose a little pace – and he was pretty sharp for a long time – he more than made up for that by applying his accumulated knowledge of a batsman's weaknesses with greater control and variation. He was a complete bowler.

Michael Holding has the grace, athleticism and ease of movement that would have ensured his place in cricket history even without many of his magnificent bowling spells. He has been called the Rolls-Royce of fast bowlers or 'Whispering Death'; so smooth and quiet is his run-up that when he first appeared in England umpires were known to look round for him because they could hear no footfall. He produced that much-discussed over to Geoff Boycott in Barbados which many people think was the fastest they ever saw. It was certainly very quick indeed, nasty and decidedly uncomfortable, not least for Geoffrey.

Michael is a beautiful bowler to watch and, as does Lillee, ensures a certain alertness and apprehension in the mind of every batsman who opposes him. I have no doubt he would have been a world-class athlete had he remained a runner. In the summer of 1984, after several strains and injuries, he cut down his run-up and there were whispers that he was fading. But even then, if he or Clive Lloyd thought it necessary, he was capable of going back to his old run; to push himself off the sightscreen as it were, to bowl with almost his old speed. For someone who is supposed to be past it, Michael has just had several good Test series against both England and Australia. Holding has been the fast bowler who has managed to get out top batsmen, consistently, on flat pitches. That takes speed and technique.

Malcolm Marshall is currently the fastest West Indian. He manages one awkward delivery that comes at you from a different angle than most and another that tends to skid on to the batsman. It's easier for batsmen to pick up a ball delivered with the high classical action of someone like Holding. Bowlers like Marshall, or Colin Croft, are often more difficult because their action precludes the earliest sighting and, as I keep emphasising, playing fast bowling is all about time. Malcolm is now the West Indies' principal strike weapon and deserves the attendant status and kudos. He is a fierce competitor, never likes his team to lose and is a good old-fashioned professional in the sense that he always knows his current performance figures. I would also defend him from much of the criticism fired at him, and the other West Indians, during the summer of 1984.

Our pitches, by and large, are simply not quick enough to tempt a fast bowler to use the bouncer very often. When he does bang it in the ball rarely lifts high enough or fast enough to become a danger. It's true that at The Oval that summer we did at last have a surface that encouraged the 'quicks' to bang in the ball. Pat Pocock, as England's nightwatchman, was on the receiving end of the sort of treatment which did not go down too well with either press or spectators. I would like to make two points about that: a nightwatchman, by definition, has some pretensions to batting and, if he hangs about for more than 15 minutes, must expect the opposition to use all possible means to get him out. If there are too many bouncers and the law regarding intimidatory bowling is breached then the umpires are there to take the necessary action. Having said that I would add that I do think that 'Percy' got more than his fair share of bumpers on that occasion.

I have grown up with it. I think every international player now accepts that whatever number he may bat in the order he is liable to get the full treatment if he hangs around for a while. This development is not, as some might think, a confirmation of a decline in the ethics of the game, but rather a recognition of the fact that in the modern game the true 'rabbit' has all but disappeared. Almost all bowlers can bat, and especially West Indian fast bowlers! The fact that tail-enders do hold up an innings and are encouraged to do so leads in turn to some aggravation from the bowlers. Imagine the frustration of a bloke who's just bowled well and taken four wickets only to find himself, tiring a little, being kept out on the field by a number eleven who, on a flat pitch, will straight-bat for the rest of the day.

The bouncer has been part of cricket almost since the game began. Every fast bowler, from the demon Spofforth and Ernie Jones, who put one through W. G.'s beard, have used this legitimate weapon. It's up to the batsman to train himself to make the right responses at the right time and quickly enough. Playing the bouncer is, if you like, an extension of batting at an ordinary level. You cannot rely on reaction time. If you were to delay making your first move until the ball left the bowler's hand you would be late on almost every stroke you played. Top players meet quick bowling by being on the move before the ball is delivered but – and this is very important – staying balanced; you can then change that movement, backwards or forwards, or extend it in one direction, as necessary. Against a Holding or a Marshall all those adjustments have to be made, correctly, in a fraction of a second.

It can be very exhilarating. First there is a period of survival, of assessing the pace and the bounce and waiting to see what the bowlers have in stock. Even Viv Richards has to go through that period against the best bowlers. Once settled, the batsman starts to look for weaknesses in the bowling, the ball that is wide or short or overpitched and, gradually, the opportunities for scoring start to open up. What is important is that the contest takes place on what might be called an impartial surface, a pitch that helps the bowlers a little and is fast enough for the ball to come off the bat. Any imbalance, too much in favour of either batsman or bowler, makes the contest one-sided and poor entertainment.

Joel Garner is a unique physical specimen (or, at least, I thought he was until I saw Tony Gray). There are times, batting against Joel on a lively, greenish track, when you wonder, quite seriously, if you are ever going to score a ton off him unless (highly unlikely) he gives you a rank bad ball. Garner is a difficult bowler to play because of the angle and the bounce of his deliveries. As ever, you cannot accept defeat before you go out to bat so you have to find some means of scoring runs against him. Like any bowler he is going to bowl you a bad ball, erring in length and direction, now and again. Patience is no bad thing! One of his great virtues is his tremendous accuracy, as his one-day record will confirm. He began as a new-ball bowler and, in 1984, reverted to his long run and took the new ball again. He can bowl fast and, when you combine pace with his other qualities of attack, Joel Garner is an exceedingly dangerous bowler.

Colin Croft was fast and strong and seemed to be forever firing in at you from a wide angle. In the first-ever Test match in Antigua the sightscreens were simply not wide enough to accommodate Colin's delivery point on the return crease. The result was that England's batsmen had to try to pick up the ball as it left Colin's hand amid a sea of black faces and bright cottons – it wasn't easy. Right-handers found Croft especially difficult because of his ability to make a fast delivery cut away.

Another common trait to all the great West Indians

is the pride they take in their performance. On a dull morning at Southampton Malcolm Marshall had bowled on an easy-paced pitch against Derbyshire and not much had happened. At lunch Bill Alley, an umpire with a mischievous sense of humour, announced in a loud voice that a certain Derbyshire batsman was 'the best hooker I've ever seen'. Malcolm heard and in the first over after lunch gave the batsman a rather swift bouncer; he hooked and dropped the ball into long-leg's hands. Malcolm had been put on his mettle and the others could all react in much the same way if their pride or status was impugned.

Andy Roberts never touches a drop of drink, is pretty reserved but has a nice sense of humour once you get to know him. Michael Holding drinks very little but can relax, has a charming personality and loves the horses. Malcolm Marshall burns up a lot of energy on and off the field but no one could ever query his performances. Joel Garner is a very friendly man, always a delight to see and chat with. Colin Croft is the least communicative.

A word too about Wayne Daniel, a big man with a big heart who has done a marvellous job for Middlesex over the years. He really has been a diamond for them in every sense and we must be thankful, paradoxically, that West Indies have been so strong in recent years that they haven't needed to call on him too often. Sylvester Clarke falls into a similar category. He has served Surrey splendidly and in doing so has impressed on all English cricketers how much of a threat he might have been had he, like Daniel, been a regular member of the West Indies' attack.

The new generation of West Indian fast bowlers,

Courtney Walsh, Anthony Gray, George Ferris, Patrick Patterson, Winston Benjamin, Ricardo Elcock and probably 50 more I don't yet know about all have the basics: they are big, strong men, all of whom let the ball go a little quickly. They remain largely untested and as yet they have still to prove that they can let it go in the same place all the time. Walsh and Patterson look the best at the moment, Ferris having been held back a little by injury (George is a little fallible in this direction). Elcock is thought likely by some good West Indian judges to be the next great fast bowler.

What makes Imran Khan one of the great fast bowlers, before and after the stress fractures that slowed him down for a while, is his ability to swing the ball both ways. A bowler who can do that at pace is distinctly dangerous to the very best of batsmen at all times and Imran has this quite astonishing facility to make the old ball move through the air. Swing is imparted to a cricket ball by polishing one side and then releasing the ball with the shinier side on the outside of the curve. The greater the contrast in polish between one side of the ball and the other the greater, in theory, is the potential swing, hence the frantic efforts made by bowlers to maintain a shine on the ball for as long as possible. It is Imran's unique gift, for a bowler of his pace, to be able to impart swing when the shine has all but gone. I do not have to emphasise that it is alarming enough to face any ball travelling towards you at 90 to 100 mph and keeping a perfectly straight course. When the old ball begins to boomerang in its split-second journey you know, as they say, that you are in trouble.

Nor is Imran only a world-class fast bowler; he is an adept enough batsman, in defence and offence, to bat as high as four or five in a Test team. He has also been a superb fielder anywhere and, on those occasions when the Pakistanis have concentrated on cricket rather than cricket politics, an effective and successful captain. As to his speed, he was tested against most of the world's fastest, in Perth, by cameras and measuring apparatus and compared very favourably with Jeff Thomson and Michael Holding. In fact, if Imran had bowled at the stumps, as did Michael, instead of hitting the pitch short of a length, his figures might have given him first place. For all that he's a shrewd man who knows and assesses his opponents, a player any captain would want in his team. He would contend on equal terms at his best with Ian Botham as the world's premier all-rounder, a better bowler than Kapil Dev, a far better batsman than Hadlee.

Richard Hadlee is capable of bowling both quickly and nastily when in the mood – he is definitely a rhythm man. Fast bowlers are almost by definition strong men, usually big strong men. Hadlee is lean and apparently unmuscled but he does have this God-given gift; when he arrives at the crease everything is co-ordinated, the balance, the very whippy action; he always has rhythm and when he puts in the extra effort he is very swift. In addition he has beautiful control and a strong competitive instinct. He moves the ball both ways, keeps a taxing length and gives you nothing, never lets you relax, but bowls well within himself regularly because he knows he is not strong enough to maintain a long barrage. He saves himself for shorter but lethal bursts.

Richard has a good change of pace and sometimes when you think that he might try a little harder you remember he has to measure himself. Hadlee is a fine model for any young man who may feel that his stature is an obstacle to bowling quickly although it must be pointed out that his virtues include many that cannot be inculcated by any coach. A great force for Nottinghamshire and New Zealand, he can be a little taciturn and withdrawn and has said and done some strange things from time to time, just as though he suddenly tires of being considered a quiet man, but there is no doubt he is a great professional.

Kapil Dev has been the mainstay of India's attack, with all the wear and tear that involves, for so long now that I wonder at his ability to keep going. He swings the ball and tends, consequently, to be much more effective with the new ball. Recently he has been inclined to slide the ball into the right-hander, perhaps a natural consequence of passing years and slight loss of pace. Kapil is a totally natural, uninhibited cricketer who was a devastating swing bowler on his day. He might have bowled longer spells for India to greater effect, but he remains one of the cleaner hitters of the ball in the world game.

Ian Botham now has to be included among the fast bowlers. He had shown previously that he could be very quick on occasions. In 1985 he and I chatted over a change of role: we agreed that for him to be an out-and-out strike bowler, to bowl fast and aggressively, would produce the results we both wanted provided he was used in shorter spells. Six months away from cricket did Ian no harm. He had time to think a few things through, and he came back to us fired up to prove a few of his critics wrong and full of enthusiasm to have another go at the Aussies. He exploded on the Somerset scene as a batsman although I think he would agree that the number of wickets he takes for the county is rather disappointing. We were all impressed with his attitude on his return and that convinced me that the time for change had arrived. Against West Indies in 1984 we had to use Ian for long spells simply because, as our most experienced bowler, he was most likely to take wickets. Only at Lord's had he been used as the strike bowler and his brilliant performance there convinced me that his greatest value to England lay in brief bursts.

What we managed to do with Ian that summer, against the Australians, was to cast him as the spearhead and he responded by running in and bowling fast – at times as fast as anyone on either side – on often slow tracks, in shorter spells of a maximum of five to six overs. Once we had other bowlers who could provide steadiness and accuracy at the other end it became possible to confirm Ian as a specialist, which paid great dividends to England. He did the job in terms of taking wickets. Ian and I had discussed the best way to maximise his contribution to the England side on several occasions. He was in favour of bowling in shorter bursts and I was keen to use him that way but all really depended on the support bowling and it was this, in fact, that became the key to winning back the Ashes. After several experiments, hampered, as always, by injuries at critical moments, that support bowling proved to be stronger than any England has enjoyed for some years, an improvement partly explained by the end of the ban on those English players who had toured South Africa under unofficial auspices.

Richard Ellison had, as they say, come on a ton in the year since his first appearance in international cricket. He had always been willing to learn and although very little went right for him in India he had the good sense to put every item of experience to good use so that by the start of the summer of 1985 he had a much better idea of what was needed to bowl out Test-class batsmen. He had developed more aggression and increased his pace by a yard, and he became something of a handful to any batsman. His reward, and England's return for encouraging him and keeping faith, was two splendid bowling performances against Australia in the last two Tests.

The steadiness and accuracy I mentioned was also supplied in some measure by Les Taylor. He may have seemed something of a surprise choice to the public at large but he had been in the selectors' minds for some years and, in fact, had he not taken off on the rebel tour to South Africa, would have been very much in contention for an England place earlier. At that stage in his career he was probably a yard quicker than when he was eventually chosen to play for England and from all the accounts I received of the rebel tour it seems Les bowled very well out there, causing their top batsmen any number of difficulties. Les then had an unfortunate spell of injuries, including cracking an elbow in training, and had reached something of a crisis in his career at the start of the 1985 season: he knew he had either to bowl through his injuries and recapture his technique and form or, simply, give up the game, at least at first-class level. To his credit he applied himself, worked out just what he had to do to bowl properly again and, although he's lost some of the pace of three years ago, he is now experienced and aware of his capabilities. He bowled very well for Leicestershire early in the summer of 1985 and proved, in the Benson and Hedges final at Lord's, that he had the temperament to produce his best on the big stage.

Neil Foster had an unfortunate 1985 in terms of injury and minor illness but I have only to cast my mind back to his 11 wickets in Madras to recall his great potential. Neil is not physically the strongest of quick bowlers but he does have a good attitude and wants to bowl. His high action has always pleased the critics but, as with many young bowlers, it does need to be monitored to ensure he does keep the arm up there. He's nippy too – the ball really hits the bat.

Graham Dilley has had a mercurial career but deserves recognition among the fast bowlers of my time. At times he has been a genuine top-class fast bowler. On the 1981 tour of West Indies, for example, he was able to shake them up a little and hit a few helmets as a reminder that not all the quick deliveries came from a black arm. I can remember him bowling on a flat pitch at Faisalabad, just before he was injured again, when there was no doubt that England possessed a real fast bowler. I nursed high hopes through the winter of 1984–85 that Graham would reappear for Kent that spring and force his way into the team to play the Australians the following summer.

Paul Allott was another who was unfortunate to be injured at a vital time in his career, missing most of the 1984–85 winter tour. He has all the qualities of the high-class stock seam bowler: accuracy, control, movement off the seam; and is someone who has learned and developed his craft commendably since he first played for England. He bowled well against West Indies in 1984 but a year later he appeared to have lost a little of his pace off the pitch. He bowled steadily enough when selected and if I say he was unlucky not to have taken more wickets then I might well be summing up his career. Paul was superseded in the side not because he had bowled badly or had let the side down in any way but because the feeling grew that he was not going to take the wickets that were needed.

Jonathan Agnew has had, to put it mildly, a career of ups and downs. He has bowled remarkably well at times but has been unable to achieve consistency. At his best he has been genuinely fast and has moved the ball late away from the bat. He also bowled well at Leicester (I can think of a performance against Kent that was of the highest quality) and leaves the impression of a player who is still learning and whose best years are still ahead of him.

Bob Willis has been a great servant to England. He has made one hell of an effort, almost alone for ten years; another good example for someone who wants to be a fast bowler. Bob underwent several setbacks; operations, physical problems, bits falling off here and there; but he worked very hard on fitness, something anyone aspiring to follow him should copy. He has good control: a common denominator of all the great fast bowlers is that even when they drop pace, or lose it, their control of length and line remains. They can still cramp the batsman, give him no room to hit and no room to nick and nudge and, at the same time, prevent him becoming complacent, still delivering the odd venomous delivery to make sure he doesn't go to sleep.

Bob struggled a little over the past two years, perhaps never being completely fit, and yet whatever work he put in always won respect. He is a genuine quick bowler, his awkward action not diminishing his ability to produce an awkward bounce, very often from an awkward angle. His general line is incoming to the right-hander and, of course, away from the left-hander but the direction of the Willis attack is only one of many threats the batsman faces: there is always a spiky hostility about Bob Willis's bowling. After I got to know him I greatly appreciated his worth as a man and a fellow player. His very strong opinions on almost anything are balanced by an excellent sense of humour, and he also has very definite views about right and wrong, a very moral man. I don't think Bob enjoyed the captaincy too much. He found it very hard work but watching him work through it increased my respect and admiration for the man.

It is a common assumption, and a mistaken one, that Mike Brearley left his successors to the England captaincy a bank of the lore of leadership from which regular withdrawals could be made. It doesn't work like that. I have never been able to say to myself: 'Now what would "Brears" have done in a situation like this?' Nor, I imagine, could Bob Willis. Each captain has his own problems to resolve, his own situations to face, his own decisions to make. By and large, Mike Brearley got them right, which makes him a great captain. There was much more to it than that, of course. Mike knew the game and knew the players, and always put that knowledge to good use in forming his judgements in making decisions. He certainly appeared to have a phenomenal memory for opposing players. He brought his intelligence to bear in an almost academic fashion in his deliberations on the cricket field, and at that stage of my career I was quite happy to accept without too much question all that happened under his control.

Was it Napoleon who said he would prefer a lucky general to a good one? Mike Brearley was also fortunate in that he led a good England team at a time when several other countries fielded weaker sides for a variety of reasons. I hope I am making a relevant point here for I have no wish to sound churlish about a man and a captain who had such a great influence on my own career. Indeed, Mike in his own book on captaincy happily admits that luck also helps the captain fulfil his schemes. I would add that it does no harm either to pick up ideas from one's colleagues during a match, discard them if necessary, but employ them if suitable. Again Mike must have agreed at least to some extent: remember Headingley in 1981, when Australia needed 130 to win and Bob Willis wanted to change ends and come downhill from Kirkstall Lane. Brearley thought it was a good idea – Willis took 8 for 43. Australia were bowled out for 111 and England won by 18 runs to record one of the most famous victories in history.

It is important, too, that a captain has the ability to bring each individual player up to his best, his maximum performance. Brearley appeared to be successful in this respect since Ian Botham was usually at his best under Mike and one of the fundamental rules all England captains have accepted in the last decade is that when Botham is playing well England are usually successful. I like to think my understanding with and of Ian has grown through my own period of captaincy – I certainly didn't complain about his 31 wickets against the Australians!

PART III

'*Passions spin the plot;
we are betrayed
by what is false
within*'

George Meredith

SPIN BOWLERS

I have a favourite spinner and am not ashamed to confess my partiality to the work of Phil Edmonds. He has had an extraordinary career of ups and downs caused partly, perhaps, by the fact that he is a highly intelligent man, possibly too intellectual for many people to accept. Philippe has more theories than most opposing teams can assemble between them. He is a keen believer in a bowler changing his field as often as possible and is prone to giving the batsman more credit than he probably deserves. He is also a genuine spinner of the ball and his control and versatility make him the best we have.

Edmonds is an aggressive bowler (and not just in terms of slipping in the odd bouncer!) in that he is always trying to bowl the perfect ball, a laudable ambition which sometimes leads to the odd bizarre delivery. But over the last 12 months he has certainly been the most controlled of our bowlers. I am very happy to take the responsibility for restoring him to the England team and was always prepared to deal with any fears or doubts there may have been about 'Henri's' individualism. Over the years I have liked and respected him as an opponent and as a colleague and, finally, was delighted to have him in my England team.

Of course he has his foibles: he has moments of irrational behaviour and when he does have one of these spells I believe in leaving him alone until it passes and we can start again. He is such a talented cricketer and all-round source of strength to the team that I can happily contend with the occasional flash of temperament. There are times when, with four men close around the bat, he will suddenly slip in a chinaman which tends to be erratic, and the reaction of Mike Gatting and his men resembles that of a Bomb Disposal Squad.

Philippe would have had many more England caps but for Derek Underwood, for so long a model of consistency and accuracy for Kent and his country. 'Unders' or 'Deadly' is rightly a legendary character. As long as I have been playing this game he has been the subject of dressing-room conversation: 'Deadly on a turner' is a phrase that is as much a part of the game as 'MCC at Lord's'. As with all legends, Derek grows to fill the mind, especially that of the young batsman who, going out to face him for the first time, is already psychologically conditioned to expect the worst, fearful that the ball will do something alarming and unexpected no matter how flat the track. Underwood is, in the current phrase, a one-off, in that he has always been that little bit quicker than his type and as such is possibly unique in the history of the game. I think Derek would have been a great bowler even without that extra pace because he has always been a true craftsman, forever varying his deliveries in length and line and speed so that a batsman's eye, judgement and reflexes are tested with every ball he receives.

Some batsmen have a good record against him. My

old colleague and friend Brian Davison would sweep Derek to death but that shot, especially against Unders, is not for ordinary mortals. Another facet of this great bowler is his temperament; even on those very rare occasions when someone like Davison got hold of him he was never ruffled, just walked back to his mark, thinking up the next delivery, confident that he would succeed in the end, as he usually did. An amiable man is Deadly, good company, a bowler who never flags, rarely stops and who has been a godsend to every captain he has served.

Both Edmonds and Underwood have impressive career figures which would have been even better, I suppose, had they bowled on uncovered pitches throughout their first-class careers. Whether the game, and in particular the Britannic Championship, would benefit from exposing the pitches again is debatable. I am certainly an opponent of change. In fact I would open the debate further by advocating four-day Championship matches. Uncovering pitches is proposed to give the spinners more opportunity, but this has not always proved to be the case in the past. A spinner may still be left out of the side chosen to play a three-day game on an uncovered pitch because the pitch may so obviously favour three or four seam bowlers.

It's true that a captain would tend to select a spinner more often than at present, as an insurance against the pitch's behaviour later in the game, but it's also true that in English weather seam and swing are usually the major weapons and the spinner might not be called upon. If the primary purpose of the county clubs, apart from winning the Championship of course, is to supply England with high-class players, then uncovering pitches might be a severe handicap. We hope to teach and train young spin bowlers to perform, at Test match level, on flat, dry surfaces because I cannot imagine that the authorities anywhere will agree to uncovering Test pitches again. We could end up training horses for the wrong courses. And there can be no real argument for uncovering Test pitches; too much then depends on the toss. Suppose England and Australia reach The Oval at 2–2, the captain winning the toss bats to reach 500, it rains all day on Sunday and the side batting second hasn't a chance. That could not be a fair Test match of skills.

John Emburey took a longish time to find his stage, starting at The Oval and then spending years waiting for Freddie Titmus to retire from the Middlesex team. Perhaps it did him no harm, for patience and a calm and practised approach to bowling are attributes of all the great spinners. By the time John actually reached the first-class game he was already a very capable performer with a fine natural action, good control and a variety of gentle changes that are the connoisseur's delight: delicate alterations to pace and flight that may go unnoticed but can prove fatal to the unwary. Perversely, he often bowls better on flat surfaces as though he enjoys testing the batsman, and getting him out, in his own environment. It's as though Embers likes to be a Daniel in the lions' den, and I'm not talking about a visit to Millwall.

One of the joys of contemporary cricket has been to watch Edmonds and Emburey bowling in tandem for both Middlesex and England. They are totally different characters from distinctive backgrounds with highly contrasting outlooks, but they complement each other remarkably well and provide great reassurance to both

Mike Gatting and myself in that we have their manifold skills to call upon in any number of permutations. The return of Emburey from his three-year suspension after South Africa, and the re-establishment of Edmonds meant that during the summer of 1985 I had almost every possible variety of bowling at my disposal. This gave us the opportunity to give each incoming batsman a thorough examination that not only exposed known weaknesses but often uncovered others previously well-hidden.

By the time we reached the second half of the series against Australia I had almost every bowling option I needed: Botham for pace, Les Taylor for control and accuracy, Richard Ellison to swing the ball and two spinners with complementary styles. Emburey's return meant, of course, that Pat Pocock had to give way again and I think the England dressing-room was sad to see him go. He deserved more England appearances as he demonstrated with his long, fine service to Surrey. As an off-spinner Pat was a little unorthodox in that he tended to experiment more than most of his type. Like the Middlesex pair 'Percy' is a brilliant craftsman.

Nick Cook, my Grace Road team-mate now with Northamptonshire, had a disappointing 1985. He swept into the England team, taking wickets at such a rate that he appeared to be a permanent fixture, but then fell away again. Nick's career has confirmed what I was saying about pitches in three-day cricket. At Leicestershire I often had to leave him out of the side in order to play the extra seamer and the lack of opportunity clearly affected his form. Nick Cook can bowl and I'm hoping that his winter tour with the England 'B' team and his move to another county, bowling with

Roger Harper at the other end, will spark him off again.

Australia have one spin bowler close to being a great exponent: leg-spinner Bob Holland. The England team ran into him when they played Northern New South Wales. He always bowled well and gave us a great deal of trouble, but he could never get into the state side, a curious blind spot of the local selectors. Not until he had reached his mid-thirties did New South Wales recognise his quality and once he had joined the side he helped them to the Sheffield Shield, won his Australian cap and then skittled West Indies at the Sydney Cricket Ground, proving the point – especially in the case of spin bowlers – that if you are good enough age is of little consequence.

Leg-spinners are so rare in English county cricket that our batsmen tend to take a while to make contact. So Bob, like Qadir before him, began well in the shires and did a fine job in the Lord's Test for Australia. He then found, like many visitors, that English pitches rarely provide the bounce and pace needed for an overseas leg-spinner to be effective. This was especially true in the forever damp summer of 1985 when so many of the surfaces the Australians played upon were either slow or dead or both. I know Bob was very disappointed not to play against England at The Oval where, at least, he could have expected to have won a little bounce even if the turn had been minimal. The relative merits of Australia's other spinners in 1985, Murray Bennett and Greg Matthews, were hard to judge because of their limited exposure in the unpromising English conditions, but both have performed well in Australia, especially at Sydney, and we could be meeting them all again fairly soon.

Both West Indies and Australia base their attack on pace, so the arrival of a new spinner from the Caribbean is always an event. England first met Roger Harper, then a gawky 18-year-old, as a member of the West Indies' President's XI, at Pointe-a-Pierre, Trinidad, during the 1981 tour when he was little more than a highly promising apprentice. Since then he has become the specialist spinner in the West Indian team, and his height gives his line of attack on awkward angle and high bounce. In 1984–85 he made a great advance – bowling as he did many overs for Northamptonshire under a sympathetic captain, Geoff Cook, Harper's accuracy and control have greatly improved. He can now give the ball a real tweak and as that ball is often delivered, in the batsman's sight, from over the top of the sightscreen, he can be quite a handful. What is especially impressive about Roger's play is his fielding. The West Indies regard him as the best fielder in the world in any position but it is in fielding to his own bowling that he has made the greatest impression on the opposition. He covers such a wide arc so quickly that the rest of his field can be that much tighter and he is brilliant in the taking of his return catches.

The best leg-spinner in the world at present (December 1985) is Abdul Qadir of Pakistan. He not only has the greatest variety of deliveries, he also exercises the greatest control over his exotic collection. He is always trying to bowl out the batsman and if he has a fault it is that he would overall return better figures by attacking less and winning more victims by luring them to their own downfall. On his day Abdul Qadir can put any batsman in the world under pressure and would have done, I suspect, in any age. He has the entire range open to the right-arm wrist-spinner.

Apart from the orthodox leg-spinner, googly and top-spinner he has several variations on each delivery including at least three different googlies – at least, that's what they tell me – I am not always convinced it is possible to bowl three different ones! There may never have been a spin bowler with so many weapons in his armoury. Having praised him to the skies it will sound immodest if I add that I enjoy playing against him and I think he enjoys the challenge, too. The game becomes a battle of wits. Qadir is a bubbly character, a happy-go-lucky man who knows he is a good bowler and delights in expressing his talents but always gives full credit to batsmen who manage to play well against him.

India's brilliant young Sivaramakrishnan is a very different character. Siva is a moody bowler. When things go his way he can be anything from a very effective to a great bowler. He is subtle and flexible, but does not offer as much variety as Qadir. Siva had an incredible start to the last series against England in India, taking 18 wickets in the first three innings but only another five in the remainder of the series. This is partly explained by the fact that the England batsmen got to know him – there were times when Mike Gatting shelled him all over the sub-continent – and also partly by the fact that he simply wasn't experienced enough to know what to do next when things went wrong. In that mood he would be better not to bowl. No doubt it is something that experience and maturity will help solve.

But Siva certainly had a magic start. His first wicket was a full toss, hit straight back at him by Graeme Fowler, and he then bowled well to earn at least some of that extraordinary success. One explanation of Siva's decline after the first two Tests might be that England batted a great deal better as the series progressed. Just as true was that, unlike on the previous tour under Keith Fletcher, the snicks went to hand and the catches were held.

Ravi Shastri, who has shared so much of India's spin bowling in recent years, is the steady, nagging type of slow left-arm bowler who aims to induce error. He does have variations and he can give the occasional delivery extra spin but he is much less of an attacker than his recent partner Siva. Partly because of India's needs, developments forced by the spread of one-day cricket, Ravi has become more of a batsman who bowls than a specialist bowler. He's a shrewd cricketer and an ambitious man and, as he has already captained India at youth level, I fully expect to see him leading his country before long. He is a single-minded cricketer with the ability to switch on and off; no one plays with more determination on the field and few can relax as well as he does off it.

PART IV

'All The Bright Company'

Julian Grenfell

1985 TOUR
AND TEST SERIES

History puts a gloss on most things: once the end result is known the original doubts and fears dwindle into insignificance. When Allan Border's Australians arrived in England in 1985 I was captaining Leicestershire at Oxford where the University were struggling on a poor surface in the Parks. At dinner one night a cheerful waiter asked me how the forthcoming series would go and I replied with something like: 'It will be close – the two sides are very evenly balanced'.

And so they were in May 1985. England's batting was the stronger, possessing greater depth and far more experience and ability in the top six, while Australia had the stronger attack in terms of pace: Lawson was the best fast bowler on either side, on current form, while McDermott was the up-and-coming threat who had already done well against West Indies; Thomson, we thought, would still have fire to offer, especially as this would be his last tour. We would certainly never underestimate him.

By contrast, in our camp there was great uncertainty about our seam attack. Whatever combination England arrived at we felt it must be inferior in terms of pace, but we did have the better spinners and we did have Botham to return to the team after missing the winter tour, rejuvenated, we hoped, and fired up again. Border and Wessels we saw as the major obstacles in Australia's batting with minor problems being posed by three or four of their younger and less experienced players, of whom Wayne Phillips was to prove outstanding.

The First Test at Headingley put us under fire a little but we came through to win. It certainly wasn't the best cricket of the series in that the bowling of both sides could have been improved, but the match did confirm our original assumptions as to the strength of our batting compared with the bowling. A win by five wickets was a good start to the series for England because the Australian bowling was haphazard enough to lift our spirits and to suggest that their quick bowlers might be less formidable than they appeared. Nor, it must be added, did the English provide their bowling performance of the year.

Lord's, however, turned the series upside-down. This was the one time in the series when England batted poorly; we left ourselves short of runs on the first innings and were unable to make up the deficit, bravely as Gatting and Botham batted in the second. Australia, in the fourth innings, collapsed to a degree. England's spinners performed well but we simply did not have enough leeway to turn the match into another escapist victory. Australia won by 4 wickets. To bounce back to 1–1 was exactly what the Australians needed to restore their morale and it reinforced the general opinion that the series was neatly balanced. Once a team does slip behind in a five- or six-match series it is imperative that that team gets on level terms as quickly as possible as the task becomes harder with each passing day. The moment time is added to the pressures exerted on a team desperate for victory it means that there is another mountain to climb.

We then entered two Test matches where conditions favoured the bat, where there was no pace for any of the bowlers, be it the Australian quicks, our spinners or Ian Botham. No one found any real encouragement in the next ten days of international cricket. The danger in these situations is that there is always the temptation for a team to allow the game to drift: five days seems a very long time in which to play out a draw. The job has still to be done, though, and the batsmen still have to bat properly. It is always possible in cricket, on the blandest of surfaces, for things to happen very quickly, which is why it is vital never to allow your concentration to slip. Trent Bridge, for instance, saw England on their way to 400 for 2 but lose their remaining wickets for less than 100 and, suddenly, everything went Australia's way: every ball in the air went to a fielder. The match ended in a draw.

At Old Trafford there was another draw. McDermott had his personal triumph while England achieved their objective, almost, but by a different route to the one planned. On the first day there wasn't the help in the pitch that I had anticipated for our bowlers so it was a good performance, especially from the England spinners, that dragged the match round. England were dominant for the last two days and on the Monday two or three semi-chances, that might have been taken with a little more keenness or a little more luck, were missed, so Australia entered the last day only 4 down instead of perhaps 7. On the last day all the credit must go to Allan Border for a great, fighting, defensive innings which, with support from Greg Ritchie, saved Australia.

Edgbaston then proved, in practice, some of my theories about the two previous Test matches. Again, conditions favoured the bat all the way through, but all a game of cricket needs to change the odds very rapidly and dramatically is for a bowler to have a purple spell, two or three batsmen to get it wrong, and a pre-ordained draw can become a sensational victory. On the Saturday morning at Edgbaston the pundits, with general agreement, had concluded that another draw was likely if not probable. But instead of a prolonged resistance from the Australian tail eating into the remaining time, 2 wickets fell in the first over and the innings was over in five minutes, a total turnaround which could almost have been measured in seconds.

Those five minutes, looking back, were the pivot of the series because from that moment onwards everything went right for England. Allan Border felt that Manchester was the psychological turning-point as Australia just hung on, but until the Saturday morning at Birmingham there must always have been a slight doubt as to whether England could win. England batted splendidly through the better part of the next two days to establish a totally commanding position and the question then became one of whether, with the pitch still perfect, there was enough time remaining to bowl Australia out. Richard Ellison bowled brilliantly, and taking 4 Australian wickets by the close on the fourth day was far more progress than we had anticipated. There was an overwhelming sense of change, of a decisive shift having occurred. That Monday night at Edgbaston will be remembered as the moment when England knew they could regain the Ashes.

The Australians had fought back characteristically at Old Trafford and were still able to surprise us with some very hostile bowling on the second day at The Oval, but that was a counter-attack by an army in retreat. A Test series, especially a six-match series, is a long time to play cricket and the simple fact is that the Australians were worn down by continuous English pressure. For a while it seemed that the weather at Edgbaston might again sufficiently reduce our available bowling time to allow another Australian escape. Even when play restarted Ritchie and Wayne Phillips again resisted valiantly and it must have been a bitter disappointment to Allan Border that his tail-enders were unable to apply themselves for long enough to baulk England.

By the end of the first day at The Oval the feeling in the England dressing-room was that the series was sewn up. Then came that last great Australian rally, on the Friday morning, to shatter any complacency and, ironically, to perk up Ian Botham and our spinners. The Oval pitch had pace and bounce and if the Australians didn't use it properly on the Thursday they did demonstrate its possibilities to our attack the following morning. England's attack then ended beautifully, each bowler playing his part exactly to the team's requirements. That Oval match was a source of considerable satisfaction to myself as the captain. I felt that the team had demonstrated the balance, strength, character and temperament we had been seeking. We had a team of winners. Personally it had been the most productive summer of my career. I felt that I had played better at times in previous seasons without scoring as many runs. One example was in Australia during the previous tour when I believe I played as well as at any time in my career in a fairly up-and-down series.

All these comparisons were a stark contrast to my form and mood at the start of the summer of 1985 when, frankly, I was worried about my inability to settle into a big innings. I was hitting the ball well enough but I had some difficulty in getting into my stride that began to nag at my confidence. In the end I became concerned enough without, I hope, showing it too publicly, to have a word with my county vice-captain and England colleague Peter Willey. On his advice I altered my stance a little, turning fractionally more square when I took guard, taking a tiny step in the direction in which 'Will' had taken a long stride several seasons before!

Peter is a very shrewd observer of cricket; he is very perceptive with a good memory and collects the bits and pieces of the game, the characteristics and idiosyncrasies of players that others simply do not notice. His advice is sound and he is rarely wrong on cricketing matters. The adjustment was so fractional that I doubt if anyone else noticed, but I immediately felt more settled, comfortable and effective. I seemed to have given myself a little more leeway when facing the bowler and, all things considered, it meant that my confidence came flooding back. It's called being in the right place at the right time.

All this did not happen overnight. I had to 'work in' the new stance, as it were, in matches and practice and there were still failures: no batsman who has ever lived has not had a run of nothing more than bad luck. I felt that I was starting to come good at Lord's where the luck was with me – one or two nicks, a drag past the keeper a couple of times and, although I missed a few, I managed to keep going. Once through that stormy start I settled into the summer. Of course I had been irritated by the criticism, by the accusations of lack of concentration and of not using my feet. I accept that my critics were looking for a rational explanation for a loss of form; there had to be reasons and it was their duty to give the public the whys and the wherefores.

The difficulty is that there isn't always an easy explanation. If you nick a ball to the keeper you are not moving your feet; if you cream it through the covers it's a glorious shot. Something which will forever stick in my mind is the chastisement I received after nicking McDermott through to Phillips a couple of times and then being accused of not moving my feet. I played a shot off Lawson, at the start of my innings at Nottingham, with my feet at least two feet away from the ball. It flew through covers, smacked against the boundary boards – the commentators described it as 'glorious' and the stroke must have been replayed ten times over on television over the next few days. Technically that shot was worse than those I had played when I had been dismissed! The difference was I hit the ball cleanly. At Test match level the margin between playing well and playing poorly can be very narrow indeed. Of course, the placing of the feet does make a difference but it is often a question of the timing of a movement rather than the movement itself.

My improvement in form rose directly from that moment when I began to move more freely and quickly to the ball and that I put down to the change in stance. I had been fractionally late with things and that split second, at Test level, can mean the difference between form and failure. Form is not entirely subjective. Few big innings are played without a fraction of good fortune, the snick that dropped just short, the catch that was missed. To go back to the start of this book, a batsman needs to make only one error for everything to go wrong. Putting the whole package together, all it takes is a little luck, a slight adjustment to technique, perhaps a less than hostile high-class attack and suddenly the confidence returns. That in turn dismisses that slight hesitation about moving to the ball which is a certain sign of weakened self-assurance. I don't need to emphasise that the quicker the bowling the less time you have to adjust.

While I was pondering upon my own form and technique I had also to think about that of my fellow England players. Graham Gooch, with one fifty and two hundreds in the Texaco matches was never a worry; he was playing well for Essex, no one could suggest he was off form and although he didn't get the scores he would have liked early in the series he certainly finished in true Gooch style. He may have been inhibited a little by the fact that his record against Australia was rather poorer than might have been expected from a batsman of his class and his desire for a really big score may have made him over-anxious at the start of the series.

Paul Downton came under criticism but never once lost the confidence of his captain. Paul is an intelligent man and a very talented batsman and wicket-keeper, or wicket-keeper and batsman, should anyone wish to read significance into the order of his place in the team. In India, Paul rapidly assumed a senior position in the team and in the dressing-room, a seniority that was needed in a largely young and inexperienced side and which was welcomed by the other members. He 'kept' well in India and batted very successfully.

He didn't have the best of summers in 1985. His batting went through a lean period while a couple of errors with the gloves were highlighted, as they were bound to be considering the amount of media attention now given to any England-Australia series. At times like that you have to draw upon your own reserves of confidence, your inner strengths, your knowledge of your own ability and hope that, with the support of friends and colleagues in the dressing-room, you will pull through. Knowing what Paul can do and having faith in that ability I tried to do for him what other players in the past have done for me when I've been going through a lean spell. I assured him that I was happy with his place in the side and left him to it. I know he would have been more concerned about his form than he would have been about criticism he received in the press, although not as much as some cricket writers suggested he should have been. Much of the criticism of his batting was undeserved and the flak he took for missed chances was to be expected, but they were slim chances. I have to confess I became a good deal angrier about what appeared to be a concerted campaign to get Paul out of the team than I ever did about criticism of my own batting or leadership. I have a lot of time for and faith in Paul Downton.

What perturbs me about the occasional wave of criticism that hits a player is that, despite any assurances that may be made to him personally, he may start to believe it all himself, consequently suffering a further loss of confidence and form until the point is reached when it becomes merciful to leave him out of the side.

More than a few Australian players have suffered in that way and more than a few have slipped from sight as a result. The self-debate that rages within a player at such a time can be debilitating in itself. The thought that runs through the mind is 'OK, I know the skipper's on my side but what are the selectors thinking?'. On the issue of Paul Downton's place in the side there may have been, for all I know, some discussion, even argument, among the selectors but they were good enough to back my judgement saying, in effect, 'If you are happy then so are we'.

The relationship between the selectors and the England captain depends a great deal on the temperaments of those individuals involved. For a successful partnership to develop there has to be trust in and loyalty to one another's judgements and total adherence to a decision once it has been made. I cannot pretend there have not been disagreements, particularly in 1984 against the West Indies. There were times then when I was overruled and in retrospect I have to say that on those occasions the selectors were mostly right and I was wrong. I had more of my own way in 1985 but by then I had a successful tour of India behind me and I could speak of the form and eligibility of players with much more authority.

It is not an easy job, picking a team, particularly the last place when there are often several options of equal value. This is when the captain may find himself out-gunned simply because the selectors have seen more of the players under discussion. I can say that all my meetings with the selectors were fairly amicable and when there has been a disagreement there has been no shouting, no marchings out of the room or banging of doors. The present system of administering the England team comes under fire from time to time, especially when England are losing Test matches, but my own experience tells me it would be hard to improve upon it. Of course there will be weaknesses if you appoint the wrong captain or the wrong selectors or both! But in any one period there should be enough true and wise men on the TCCB to see that this doesn't happen often, if at all. I cannot believe that appointing an England team manager would be an improvement.

I would strongly resist any diminution of the captain's authority. Cricket is a game in which managers, as on tour, are there to assist in taking the pressure off the captain in organisational matters, to give good advice and support on all subjects including cricket but not to interfere in any way with the captain's command of his ship, that is the team and the cricket. What precisely would an England team manager do? His position would mean that he would have to be with the England team at all times and therefore see even less of county cricket and of possible candidates than the present four selectors. If the selectors were retained as talent scouts who forwarded their recommendations to the manager – who, presumably, would have the last word on team selection, otherwise his position would be untenable – the result would be the highly illogical, not to say comical, situation in which an England team could take the field wanted neither by the selectors nor the captain.

Comparisons with other sports are invalid. In no other sport does international play take up a third of the entire season, making the selection process difficult and continuous. A squad system is not the answer either, for cricket is one game in which an unknown in May can be famous by August. The present system has its faults but it is a good old British compromise and works well on the whole. The captain and the four selectors all have their own way of taking soundings, by speaking to other captains or senior players, umpires or simply people whose judgement they respect. Cricket is really a very democratic institution – the groundsman at Hinckley may know more about and have sounder views upon some facet of the game than, say, the Secretary of MCC. Cricket has always had a very fertile grapevine. Not much happens in Canterbury that isn't known in Edgbaston or Bradford by the following day. And with every hilarious story that may float through the bar of an evening there is usually a good idea or two and a valuable judgement. It's part of the joy of the game.

The development of a cricketer, from county player to Test level, is helped by a widening of experience which is why I welcomed the tour of the England 'B' team last winter. Bowling in Sri Lanka was a useful exercise for Jon Agnew, Nick Cook and David Lawrence; all three, we hope, have returned as candidates for the full England team, thus adding to the number of options open to the selectors. Match-winning Test teams are built on a strong, deep reserve of first-class bowlers which is why West Indies have been supreme for so long: as soon as one great fast bowler has ended his career, two more are vying for his place.

Several times, in the summer of 1985, the Australian media were hyper-critical of English pitches and the suggestion was made that England had somehow contrived the slow surfaces deliberately to negate the

Australian fast attack. That, of course, is nonsense. The TCCB can ask groundsmen to prepare quicker pitches but no one has the authority to order slower ones. It should have been obvious, even to the Australian media, that the amount of rainfall that summer throughout the country would have made it extremely difficult for any groundsman to produce a hard, flat surface. England won back the Ashes principally because whenever the Australians did bowl badly, for whatever reason, Lawson's fitness or McDermott's inexperience, England's batsmen were good enough to take advantage of the opportunities offered.

Australia's batsmen, Border apart, were never able to dominate England's much more varied and accurate attack. Wessels had a poor time against the spinners, and Wood had one good innings. Ritchie batted well enough to suggest what he might have achieved in a successful side and of the others only Wayne Phillips showed any real consistency. How much better Australia would have been had Kim Hughes and his South African 'rebels' been available must be a matter for conjecture; there is no guarantee that the Australian selectors would have regarded too many of the 'rebels' as potential English tourists in much the same way that only Gooch and Emburey were the certain and definite losses to England during their three-year suspension. I need hardly add that England were quite happy to see an Australian team arrive without Hughes and Terry Alderman.

England's rebuilding had started before the return of our two stalwarts when a whole school of candidates were put through the fire of the 1984 series against West Indies. Some were brought back, like Chris Tavaré, others were thrown in at the deep end, like Chris Broad. Graeme Fowler stuck it out nobly through that summer, which proved to be a traumatic experience for some, starting with Andy Lloyd, who had made a lot of runs for Warwickshire in the two previous seasons, had been highly recommended and had made a good start to the season. Andy had earned his place in the side and then played confidently and steadily through the Texaco Trophy matches. He looked the part and was playing the West Indians reasonably well. Then, on the first morning of the match at Birmingham, he became casualty number one and the whole series started on the wrong note.

England then turned to Martyn Moxon who became the second casualty. He was injured in a county match after selection but before he could play in a Test match. The next one to be called up was Chris Broad, who fitted in well, stood up to the quick bowlers, displayed the right temperament and did all that was asked of him through the summer. Not to have been selected for the tour of India must have been a nasty shock for him, but at least the selectors can take some pleasure in the results of his replacement Tim Robinson, who performed so very well through the tour and then against Australia. Mike Gatting, not in the best of form, returned for the Second Test, an excellent match for England until the last four hours, which turned it into the worst day of the series. At Leeds, for the Third Test, Paul Terry came in to bat number three, and Paul Allott was back in attack. Terry was retained for Manchester where England tried another spinning combination, Cook and Pat Pocock, the two spinners being fielded in the belief that there might be some turn in the

Old Trafford pitch. Bob Willis's Test career ended and Norman Cowans was restored.

By the time England reached The Oval, 4–0 down, the search for a team that could win was still paramount; any thoughts of India and the one-day tournament in Australia at the close of the winter tour were very secondary. Yet at The Oval further experiments brought in Agnew and Ellison, selections that must have been conditioned by the knowledge that England would tour India without either Willis, who was to retire, or Botham, who had already withdrawn. England's two leading wicket-takers of the previous five years would both be missing. Another defeat meant a true nadir for England, and in the additional Test match that season, against Sri Lanka, fielding the team that played at The Oval, we hardly covered ourselves in glory. Indeed, according to the media, we were rather fortunate not to have been at least burned in effigy.

There were no excuses, but I think I can offer an explanation: those of us who had played in all five Tests against West Indies (Botham, Lamb, Fowler, Downton and myself) had lived an age and a half through a long, long summer. Playing against the Sri Lankans – no disrespect to them for they played the better cricket – was so totally different that the atmosphere was more that of a festival than of a Test match. The match was, as it was meant to be, a celebration for Sri Lanka while the public were right to expect a better performance from England.

When the selectors came to choose a touring side for India they had some fairly depressing reports: apart from four days at Lord's England had been outgunned and outplayed and had not been able to settle on a team, partly because of injuries and partly through lack of form. Looking back, England probably made too many changes in an effort to find a sense of direction. The feeling of the meeting was that a sorry chapter had closed; that we had to sit back, reflect on our strengths and our weaknesses, forget all about West Indies (temporarily) and set our minds to picking a side that could win in India. There were also two one-day series to be played, in India and Australia, but these were subsidiary to the main target of beating India at home in a Test series. I am now sorry that England didn't put up a better performance in the one-day tournament in Australia because our disappointing results there, after a hard four-month tour of India, tarnished, in the public memory, so much fine work in India.

However, the immediate problem of team selection revolved around the large and alarming gap left by one I. T. Botham. When Bob Willis was England's captain his retort to suggestions in the press that Botham might be dropped was usually: 'You give me the names of the three players I will need to replace him'. The replacement in India turned out to be, to everyone's surprise, Chris Cowdrey. An old and longstanding friend of mine, Chris would never claim to be an all-rounder in Botham's class but he did have his days. He gave 100 per cent throughout, and made several more than useful contributions. Richard Ellison, too, was part of the Botham replacement plan although he had already appeared, along with Ian, in the previous Test match at The Oval.

Turning to the batsmen, Fowler was our number one opener by right of performance and seniority. The preference for Tim Robinson over Chris Broad may have been a surprise to all but the selectors, for both had been under consideration for the whole of the previous summer. Broad was marginally the favourite on the basis of his performance against West Indies, but it was thought that Robinson might be the better player in Indian conditions. Martyn Moxon, originally selected before either of the Nottinghamshire pair, although injury had prevented him proving he was a good player, made up the three. I argued very strongly for the reinstatement of Mike Gatting. He had made a lot of runs for Middlesex, played spin admirably and I believed he would be lethal against Indian-type bowling. The selectors agreed and Mike, perhaps reinforced by a further vote of confidence, never really looked back after that. The first four batsmen we chose were all winners: Fowler gave us the runs we needed and quickly, Robinson and Moxon fought all the way for second place. Martyn unfortunately had to return home temporarily to attend his father's funeral, and his absence gave Tim a lead that was never overtaken.

, After his heroic efforts against West Indies, Allan Lamb had a leaner time but still averaged 40 in India. Paul Downton, who had enjoyed a quietly effective summer, averaging 23 down the order against West Indies, had an excellent tour, contributing much to performance and morale in the field. The side was also reinforced by two top-class spinners, Pocock and Phil Edmonds. Again, I campaigned vigorously for Philippe and when it was pointed out that in the opinion of some senior figures he was regarded as a prickly character I replied: 'That's my responsibility'. I admired Philippe's ability, not only as England's spin bowler but as a batsman whose figures did not truly reflect his talent and as an expert close field. I liked him as a man, regarded him as a friend and was very confident that we could establish a successful working relationship – and so it proved.

The seam attack looked versatile and varied enough for India: Foster, Ellison and Allott, with Agnew (later to replace Allott) a borderline case, just missing the original selection. In Norman Cowans we had the fast bowler, with the versatile and adaptable Vic Marks as the reserve spinner. Bruce French was adjudged the best of the younger challengers for the number two keeper to Downton and had an excellent tour, doing all that was asked of him in an excellent spirit, fully knowing that his chances of playing would be extremely limited.

England in India were not the strongest touring party ever sent abroad but they did have many virtues in that they were good professionals, well balanced in the various requisite skills, and all of them were excellent characters who maintained morale and never lacked spirit. It will have been partly forgotten now, but the tour began in the most inauspicious circumstances. The assassination of Mrs Gandhi happened as we arrived, to be followed by the murder of an Englishman in Bombay. The England team were never in any danger and great credit must be given to Sri Lanka for their efforts in organising our short break in their country. The second murder took place in Bombay two days before the start of the first Test match, and threw everything into confusion again. The death of an Englishman prompted all kinds of speculation and fears for the safety of the team. The High Commission were reassuring and right in their assessment that no harm was intended to a visiting cricket team but there had to be misgivings. We spent some time cooped up in our hotel before the manager, Tony Brown, and myself decided to consult the High Commission again before agreeing that the best thing to do was to carry on with the tour.

The players needed practice, as much to get their minds off events as anything, and we did have a Test match to play. When that match finally began it must be admitted that most of the England players found it hard to give 100 per cent concentration to the play; in view of the circumstances it was hard to focus the mind on cricket. I won the toss and, quite rightly, elected to bat, but England ended with a disappointing first innings score of 195 when we should have reached 400 plus. When India batted, Ellison was unlucky, beating the bat several times, and having one caught off a no-ball. India were three down when it could have been four or five. As the ball aged, India settled and we then came under a lot of pressure from Shastri and Kirmani. Gatting and Downton batted well throughout England's second innings but to save the game was a tall order and we would have needed a little luck to have done it. India won by 8 wickets and it was at this point that the character of the team shone through. Fortunately, not too many of the England side had been on the previous tour when Keith Fletcher's team went down 1–0 at Bombay and were not able to get back into contention in a six-match series. Those who had been on that tour, including myself, had our misgivings but we kept them to ourselves.

I made the point to the players, immediately, that we had to bounce straight back to try to level the series knowing that, once we had jumped this hurdle, anything could happen in India and this we were able to do in Delhi. It was a tremendous recovery in that even at lunch on the last day the situation looked a little bleak, but we won the match on the last afternoon. England did exactly what had to be done. Morale played a major part in the rest of the series. India went through a lean patch until their victory in Bombay, after which another defeat plunged them, I suspect, into depression again. The momentum of the series had swung England's way.

Calcutta, I'm afraid, was a dreadful bore. We lost a day's play when India had the advantage and the fact that they weren't allowed to exploit it must have been another big disappointment. On to Madras where England played so splendidly, producing an all-round convincing performance to win by 9 wickets, and it was then that I knew for the first time that England had a team of winning potential. Foster bowled magnificently. We held catches, put India under sustained pressure and bowled them out for 272. Our first four batted superbly, Fowler and Gatting knocking up double hundreds, and although India rallied in their second innings, they were always, vainly, trying to stave off defeat. It was an all-round first-class team performance from England contending, as we had to, with Azharrudin beginning against us with 110, 48 and 105 in his first two Tests.

India exerts different fascinations (and in some instances repulsions) on each individual. Many cricketers will tell you that it is the most interesting country of them all to tour, to Western eyes a very strange and beautiful land of friendly and hospitable people, most of them, it seems, fanatical cricket lovers. There are also players who react badly to the smells and the heat and the food, and if you are feeling ill every other day then India can be a long, tiring and depressing tour. My admiration goes out to those players who, like Bruce French, know they have little opportunity of playing, unless there is an unfortunate injury, during the Tests but still contrive to make the best of it.

Bruce turned out to be our foremost explorer, forever diving off into markets and seeking out the local places of interest, always making very good use of the time of which, it is true, he was rarely short. Climbing is one of his hobbies and he made sure that he got to see Everest by making a special trip to Nepal. Tim Robinson joined me on a trip to a tiger reserve, for him a new venture that he greatly enjoyed. The whole touring party – for some it was the first time and for others the tenth – insisted on going to see the Taj Mahal, and I do not intend to sound patronising: on a long tour a rest day is not given up lightly. Coaches, trains, aircraft and taxis are all part of a working day for the touring cricketer.

Azharrudin scored another century against us in Kanpur where India built up 553 and there was a threat of an England follow-on, Edmonds helping to avert that and thus denying India their last chance. Having won the one-day series comfortably we had good reason to think we had done the job well. England flew on to Australia well satisfied; I felt we had several certain starters for the following summer, not to mention Botham's return and Gooch and Emburey being available again for selection. The programme included a week off, on arrival, for rest and re-charging which was a good idea at the time but in retrospect meant we lost our momentum. After the euphoria of winning in India, which not too many teams have achieved, it was very difficult to adjust to the razzmatazz of the World Championship of cricket. It was very hard for an English player, in those circumstances, to screw himself up into believing in the importance of the competition.

The Australian celebrations did not affect my judgement or opinion of the England players involved nor influence my preferences when I sat down with the selectors for our first task on returning home, that of naming a squad for the Texaco Trophy matches against the Australians. I could put down on paper the names of Fowler, Robinson and Gooch; Gatting, Lamb, Botham and myself; Downton; Edmonds, Emburey; Cowans, Foster, Allott, Willey and Ellison to which would be added Agnew, Taylor and Arnie Sidebottom. Sadly, we lost some on the way. Graeme Fowler began that summer in terrible form but we backed him initially because he is a good man to have around, a bouncy, resilient player, always chirpy, who loves his cricket and who is the source of great fun in the dressing-room. Bright and intelligent, Graeme has a fund of earthy Lancashire humour that has brightened many a dark day and desperate situation.

But his lack of runs and his ability to find original ways of getting out, combined with a neck injury, meant he had to be left out although, knowing him, I am sure he will be back again once he has sorted himself out physically. Graeme's departure wasn't the problem it might have been because we had the mighty Gooch ready once more while Tim Robinson, that quiet, reserved newcomer in India, had settled in as though born to the job of opening for England.

We knew all about Gooch's prowess but Tim was a surprise: he is a phlegmatic character with a dry sense of humour, an excellent professional who worked continuously at getting things right (he claims Geoffrey Boycott as his model and that has done him no harm) and who played sensibly, within his limitations but with his mind on targets.

Graham Gooch came back under a lot of pressure – he was sensitive to all the expectations – and displayed his acknowledged class and power. Allan Lamb is another class batsman who had a magnificent series against West Indies and then had a much quieter time in India, a situation which can be partially explained by his inability to come to terms with the local cuisine. He topped the list for tummy trouble on that tour.

Back in England we greet the return of I. T. Botham, whose new image gave the dressing-room unlimited scope for mickey-taking. Not that 'Both' was inhibited, nor had he changed in the slightest – you couldn't change that personality – but we all sensed that the break from cricket had refreshed him, as he soon proved against the Australians.

Peter Willey, the complete professional, the perfect strong, silent man, gives nothing away in public. In private he knows a deceptive amount about the game. He is especially astute in spotting flaws, or potential flaws, in playing techniques. I have talked batting to him, stroke production, the correct stance and so forth. He is equally knowledgeable and shrewd about bowling. During 1985, when he was out of the England team, he spent much time watching our performances on video and, for instance, was able to spot a slight difference in John Emburey's action that no one, including the bowler, had noticed. That kind of perception is invaluable. As Peter Willey is also a more than useful performer with bat or ball and one who will put his personal feelings and ambitions second to the team's needs, he is a useful man to have in the party, which is why he was booked for a second tour to the West Indies.

Les Taylor has the classical fast bowler's background of a working miner; he did actually leave the pit to bowl for Leicestershire and makes no secret of his gratitude for the opportunity to do so. But he still identifies with the life of a miner, puts his back into his work and was thrilled, when it seemed his career might be going downhill, to win an England place. Les is a country man – he loves country sports, including fox-hunting, and is very much of solid English yeoman stock, feet on the ground and no nonsense from anybody.

Why not four days?

Elsewhere I have expressed opinion on covered pitches. I am in favour of keeping the playing surfaces covered in all competitions and I believe that a further improvement in the Britannic Championship would be brought about by playing the competition's matches over four days rather than three. This would bring a reduction in the number of fixtures and an improvement in their quality: each county could field its strongest team more frequently, being under less pressure from international calls, and each county would play each other once, thus removing the anomaly of having either two fixtures against the strongest opponent, or two fixtures against the weakest.

Four-day matches of less frequency would give groundsmen more opportunity to prepare fair pitches, balanced in that they favour neither bat nor ball. Perhaps it is naive to believe that some counties would not still attempt to produce wickets to suit their own strengths, but it is essential for the idea to carry some weight that pitches be prepared properly according to TCCB guidelines. Matches over four days on fair pitches would give the captains time to make a proper contest without the third-day contrivances that have become such a feature of the Championship in recent years. Four days would mean that teams would have to maintain a higher standard of play throughout; there would be less opportunity to 'go through the motions' while waiting for a declaration to bring the game to life again on the third day.

I also believe that players' attitudes might change because 16 matches a season present far fewer opportunities than 24 for a man to make his mark. This should lead to a rise in the quality of play. And, of course, there should be more sense of occasion about a County Championship match. Eight home matches, as opposed to 12 at present, would increase the value of the currency while the loss in playing time, to supporters and members, would be just four days.

THE
PLAYGROUNDS

It is of course quite impossible to describe Lord's as a playground. Whatever one's nationality and background Lord's has an impact on a cricketer totally unlike the impression gained from any other major ground. All the cliché descriptions – the Mecca, the cathedral – are all perfectly correct: there is no place on earth quite like it. Tradition is almost tangible, especially in the dressing-rooms where, seemingly reluctantly, improvements are made from time to time, very gradually. In my time some of the old sofas, traditional chairs and seats have gone leaving pleasant memories in the minds of those who will remember the dressing-rooms as they were.

So many features contribute to the character of Lord's, even the famous slope on the pitch. There are Nancy's lunches for the players, always good grub, always another helping if you need it. Lord's was the scene of my maiden hundred, against Middlesex, as an 18-year-old before I left on an England youth tour. I also scored a century against New Zealand there and, very happily, in 1985 I was able to receive the Benson and Hedges Trophy there on Leicestershire's behalf.

Australia's equivalent to Lord's is the Sydney Cricket Ground. The old character has been eroded somewhat by the floodlight pylons, new scoreboards and the new stands, and the Hill itself has been diminished. Nevertheless the old SCG remains a very impressive stadium with the old pavilion and much of the old, green painted ironwork remaining. The new stands are possibly the best in the world – very impressive structures, providing every facility, in supreme comfort, for the spectator. Again, the old dressing-rooms lend much atmosphere to the SCG; I would guess that the fittings were used by Bradman. Those dressing-rooms have since become famous worldwide, featuring prominently in the making of the television film *Bodyline*.

To the public the Hill is what makes Sydney unique, and all England players have to take the lash from the crowd, some of it good-natured, some of it vitriolic. Geoff Boycott always had a high time under the Hill: on one occasion he was pelted with fruit and on another menaced by a gorilla or, at least, someone (not I. T. Botham) doing a suitable impersonation of one.

Up the eastern coastline of the Pacific from Sydney is the Woollongabba, Brisbane's famous ground known more regularly simply as 'The Gabba', home of great cricket and the fabulous hospitality of the Queenslanders, especially the Queensland Cricket Club. England usually call at Brisbane fairly early in the tour. It's a smaller ground than one expects in Australia but there is always a great atmosphere when England play, fierce partisanship on the field and a home from home off it. The barbecues on the Gabba, after close of play, are rightly renowned around the world.

I've enjoyed my cricket there, not least a 158 against New Zealand in the one-day World Championship. There is a greyhound track around the pitch and it has become customary to invite England to dinner one night when the dogs are running. On one occasion, as a result of local advice, Ian Botham and Allan Lamb found themselves handsomely in profit, but put all their winnings on the last race – and lost.

Edgbaston is by no means the prettiest of England's Test grounds but the facilities there are excellent, the ground is well organised and administered and no batsman could fail to be fond of a pitch upon which he scored two Test double hundreds. Alan Smith, the Warwickshire secretary, and his staff always ensure that visiting players are cared for and looked after.

Of the Caribbean grounds Kensington Oval, Bridgetown, Barbados, is the one with the most atmosphere. Cricket is paramount on the island – a shop without a radio broadcasting a Test match can expect no customers – and no effort is spared in getting a seat or a perch at the Oval. When a sightscreen was extended in 1981, the top of the right-hand corner was cut away to help the view from one of the stands. Throughout the match a mounted policeman found it necessary to be stationed there, conveniently placed to peer through and presumably keep an eye on lawbreakers in the crowd.

There was an extension to an old stand alongside the pavilion. Several hundred managed to find a perch on the tin roof of this extension during a Test match. As the day wore on and the rum took effect you could spot the odd spectator sliding off the roof and falling into a contented slumber on the ground below; it never distracted his friends from their whole-hearted participation in what was going on in the game.

The WACA (a shortening of West Australia Cricket Association) ground at Perth has won my affection for two reasons: it was the first ground I saw in Australia and I watched a lot of cricket there when I wasn't playing for the local club, Claremont-Cottesloe. I was shown a great deal of warmth and hospitality there and got to know the Australians properly. It was another warming experience to go back to the WACA ground again the following year, 1978–79, as an England player to score a hundred against Australia.

I am fond of Trent Bridge because it has a special atmosphere among English grounds: it always seems a little quieter when we play there yet there is a surge of warmth and friendliness from the crowd. Trent Bridge has been good to me as an England player – I have good memories of two innings there – but less kind to me as a county player when every year I seem to find a new means of getting out. There is always something of a 'derby' feel about Nottinghamshire–Leicestershire matches and I've taken a little gentle stick from the Nottinghamshire crowd over the years, which is fair enough – those same supporters are behind me when I play for England.

Many of us in the England dressing-room believe that Trent Bridge ought to be renamed Derek Randall Park! You can be sure that if Derek isn't in the England team when we play there we will have to field a million questions as to why not.

Adelaide is the most scenic of the Australian grounds. There is a more sedate ambience at the Oval, helped by the ivy-covered walls, the tennis courts at the back of the grandstand and, I suppose, the effort the South Australian Association puts into maintaining the Oval as a ground of beauty and distinction. The Adelaide crowd, too, have a little more dignity. Even in their wildest moments they never become as frenetic as, say, the Melbourne or Sydney spectators.

The pitch itself is remembered by players for its immense length. It is a stretched oval so to clear the boundary with a straight hit is a fair achievement. The best I can remember is a hit by Ian Botham (who else?) off Ewen Chatfield, in a one-day game, the ball soaring over long-off towards the scoreboard. It made a few old-stagers sit up, even those who probably remembered Frank Woolley (who, of course, would have hit it even further out of the ground!).

The Oval – the Surrey one, that is – is noted for qualities other than its scenery. Nowadays it has become another home ground for the West Indies because England, judging from the racket, might as well be playing in Kingston or Port-of-Spain. Surrey have a very progressive administration and I remember one of their innovations: the first provision, in England, of an electronic scoreboard that permitted video replays. Unfortunately, it was so sited as to catch the corner of the eye of a left-handed batsman and, sadly, spent much of the match unused.

The Oval has been an all-or-nothing ground for me as a player, but it has still given me more than one innings to remember. Players know it for having the best plunge bath and shower facilities in England.

Last, but a very long way from being least, in my list of the great playgrounds is Calcutta. It is impossible in any list of cricket grounds not to mention Eden Gardens, for nowhere in the world does the game consistently attract such large and knowledgeable crowds.

More than 90,000 regularly attend Test matches, the

atmosphere is electric and every player who takes the field is conscious of this attention and prays he can do well. It was such a shame, in 1984–85, that the spectators had such a dull Test match to watch; on the last day we did our best to entertain them with Allan Lamb, at third man, borrowing a policeman's helmet and stick and strutting around with them. It worked up to a point, but the Bengalis are very sporting and informed and deserve better cricket than that put before them on occasions.

Lord's, Sydney, The Gabba, Edgbaston, Bridgetown, The WACA, Trent Bridge, Adelaide, The Oval, Calcutta; no particular order, no particular preferences – just golden memories.